The Best Short Stories of
Edgar Allan Poe

by Edgar Allan Poe

Level 3
(1600-word)

Retold by Michael Brase

IBC パブリッシング

はじめに

　ラダーシリーズは、「はしご（ladder）」を使って一歩一歩上を目指すように、学習者の実力に合わせ、無理なくステップアップできるよう開発された英文リーダーのシリーズです。

　リーディング力をつけるためには、繰り返したくさん読むこと、いわゆる「多読」がもっとも効果的な学習法であると言われています。多読では、「1. 速く 2. 訳さず英語のまま 3. なるべく辞書を使わず」に読むことが大切です。スピードを計るなど、速く読むよう心がけましょう（たとえば TOEIC® テストの音声スピードはおよそ 1 分間に 150 語です）。そして 1 語ずつ訳すのではなく、英語を英語のまま理解するくせをつけるようにします。こうして読み続けるうちに語感がついてきて、だんだんと英語が理解できるようになるのです。まずは、ラダーシリーズの中からあなたのレベルに合った本を選び、少しずつ英文に慣れ親しんでください。たくさんの本を手にとるうちに、英文書がすらすら読めるようになってくるはずです。

《本シリーズの特徴》

- 中学校レベルから中級者レベルまで5段階に分かれています。自分に合ったレベルからスタートしてください。
- クラシックから現代文学、ノンフィクション、ビジネスと幅広いジャンルを扱っています。あなたの興味に合わせてタイトルを選べます。
- 巻末のワードリストで、いつでもどこでも単語の意味を確認できます。レベル1、2では、文中の全ての単語が、レベル3以上は中学校レベル外の単語が掲載されています。
- カバーにヘッドホーンマークのついているタイトルは、オーディオ・サポートがあります。ウェブから購入／ダウンロードし、リスニング教材としても併用できます。

《使用語彙について》

レベル1：中学校で学習する単語約1000語

レベル2：レベル1の単語＋使用頻度の高い単語約300語

レベル3：レベル1の単語＋使用頻度の高い単語約600語

レベル4：レベル1の単語＋使用頻度の高い単語約1000語

レベル5：語彙制限なし

CONTENTS

The Murders in the Rue Morgue............................ 1

The Black Cat 41

The Gold Bug... 61

Word List.. 116

The Murders
in the Rue Morgue

パリに長期滞在中の私は、あるきっかけがもとで没落した名家の出であるC・オーギュスト・デュパンと知り合い、場末の古びた家を借りて一緒に住み始める。ある日、二人の目に猟奇殺人の新聞記事が止まった。「モルグ街」のアパートメントの4階で二人暮らしの母娘が惨殺されたのだった。

読みはじめる前に

The Murders in the Rue Morgue で使われている用語です。わからない語は巻末のワードリストで確認しましょう。

☐ chimney
☐ choke
☐ crime
☐ doubt
☐ escape
☐ imitate

☐ institution
☐ interpreter
☐ lightning rod
☐ motive
☐ murderer
☐ nail

☐ orangutan
☐ razor
☐ sailor
☐ shutter
☐ state
☐ undertaker

用語解説

Rue Morgue モルグ街 物語の舞台となるパリの一画。フランス語で、rue は「通り」、morgue は「死体公示所、霊安室」をそれぞれ意味する。

主な登場人物

I 私 この物語の語り手。デュパンと共にパリの一画に住む。

C. Auguste Dupin C・オーギュスト・デュパン 私の友人。夜をこよなく愛し、日中は窓を閉めきって読書や書き物にふける。奇怪で残虐な殺人事件の謎を見事な推理で解いていく。なお、ポーの他の作品、『マリー・ロジェの謎』『盗まれた手紙』もデュパンが主人公で、小説に登場する初の名探偵と呼ばれる。

Madame L'Espanaye レスパネ夫人 モルグ街で起こった殺人事件の犠牲者。

Camille L'Espanaye カミーユ・レスパネ レスパネ夫人の娘。母と共に何者かに殺害される。

Adolphe Le Bon アドルフ・ル・ボン 銀行員。モルグ街の殺人事件の容疑者として逮捕される。

When I was living in Paris during the spring and part of the summer of 18__, I met a young gentleman named C. Auguste Dupin. He came from a good family, but he was now without money and had given up all hope of success in life. What money he had, he spent on books.

We first happened to meet because we were both looking for the same old book. We met many times after that. I was especially interested in his family history, and I was very much surprised by the amount of reading he had done. But more than anything, I liked his strength of mind. I would like to have him as a friend, I thought, and I told him so.

We decided to live together during my stay in Paris. Since I had more money than he did, I paid for the old house we lived in. The house was cheap because something very strange had happened there many years ago. We didn't tell

THE BEST SHORT STORIES OF EDGAR ALLAN POE

anyone where we were living, so no one came to visit us.

Dupin loved the night more than anything, and I began to love it, too. During the day, we would cover the windows so that no light could get in, and we would read and write and talk. When night came, we went out into the city and walked far and wide.

One day, we came across the following article in a newspaper:

Murder

About three o'clock this morning, the people of St. Roch quarter were woken by terrible cries. The cries seemed to be coming from the fourth floor of a house on the street called Rue Morgue. The house was that of Madame L'Espanaye and her daughter, Camille L'Espanaye.

The gate to the house wouldn't open, so eight or ten neighbors and two men from the police had to force it open. The cries had ended by that time, and the group rushed up the stairs of the house. Two voices could still be heard from further up. Soon, however, these voices stopped, and the house grew quiet.

The group spread out and hurried from room to room. Finally they came to a large room on the fourth floor. The door was locked from the inside, and they later found that the key was still in the lock. When they forced the door open and looked in, they couldn't believe what they saw.

The room looked as if it had been hit by a storm. Broken chairs and tables and clothes were thrown here and there. What had been on the bed was now on the floor. A razor was lying on a chair. It was covered with blood. Some long, gray human hair was in front of the fireplace. It seemed to have been pulled with great force from the head of a living person. It was spotted with blood. There were four pieces of gold money on the floor, as well as an earring, several silver objects, and two bags of gold money. Under the bed was an iron box, with the key in the lock. Inside the box were some old letters and papers—nothing of much value.

There was no sign at all of Madame L'Espanaye. However, there was something strange about the fireplace. When someone looked up the chimney, the body of the daughter (what a terrible sight!) was found there, hanging head down. The body was still quite warm, and there were many cuts on it, probably because of the way it had been pushed up the chimney. There were also many small cuts on the face. The neck had dark marks in the shape of fingers, as if the daughter had been choked to death.

After looking through the rest of the house and finding nothing, the group went out to the yard in back. There they found the old lady's body. Her neck had been cut all the way through, so that when they tried to lift her up, her head fell off. Both her head and her body were in such terrible condition that the old lady no longer looked human.

At the present moment, no one seems to have any idea how this all happened.

The Murders in the Rue Morgue

The next day's paper gave more information.

The Case of the Rue Morgue

Many people have been questioned about this case, but nothing important has been discovered yet. We give below what has been learned so far.

Pauline Dubourg has washed clothes for Madame L. and her daughter for three years. According to her, the two seemed to get along well together. They paid well, too. She knew nothing about how they lived. She had heard that the old lady had a great deal of money in the house. She never saw any other people there. There was no help living in the house either. There seemed to be no tables or chairs in the house except on the fourth floor.

Pierre Moreau, who deals in tobacco, has sold small amounts to Madame L. for the past four years. He was born in the area and has always lived there. The old lady and her daughter have lived in the house for six years. During those six years, he had seen Madame L. and her daughter only five or six times. The two kept very much to themselves. He had never seen any other people go into the house except for a doctor, maybe eight or nine times.

Many other neighbors spoke in much the same way. Not many visitors came to the house. No one knew if the two had any family ties besides themselves. The front windows to the house were usually closed. The ones in back were always closed except for those on the fourth floor. The house was a good house—not very old.

Isidore Musèt, from the police, explained that he was called to the house about three o'clock in the morning. He found some twenty or thirty people at the gate, trying to get in. It didn't take him long to get the gate open. The cries from inside continued until then, when they suddenly stopped. The cries had been made by a person (or persons) in a great deal of pain. They were loud and long cries, not short and quick.

When he and the others reached the second floor, they heard two angry voices. One voice was *very low, the other high and strange. The low voice was speaking French. He was sure it was a man's voice, not a woman's. He could hear the words "What the devil!" and "My God!"*

The high voice was speaking in a foreign language. He was unable to tell if it was a man or a woman. Although he couldn't understand any of the words, he believed that it was Spanish.

Henri Duval, who is a neighbor and who makes silver objects, reports that he was one of the first to enter the house. In general, he agrees with what Musèt has said. As soon as they got inside the house, they closed the door to keep the crowd from coming in. He believes that the high voice was that of an Italian. He is sure it was not French. He couldn't tell whether it was a man's or a woman's voice. He doesn't know Italian, and couldn't catch any of the words. But there is no doubt in his mind that it was Italian. He knew Madame L. and her daughter quite well, and had talked with them often. He was sure that the high voice belonged to neither of them.

———— Odenheimer, who runs a restaurant, is from Amsterdam, and does not speak French. He was questioned with the help of an interpreter. He heard the cries as he was passing by the house. They lasted for several minutes—probably ten. They were long, loud, and terrible. He entered the house with the others. He agrees with the others in every way but one. He believes that the high voice was speaking French and belonged to a man, although he could not pick out any words that he knew to be French. The words were loud and quick, not equal in length. They seemed to be spoken not just in anger, but also in fear. The low voice said the words "My God!" and "What the devil!" a number of times.

Jules Mignand, banker, reports that Madame L. owned some land. She had been doing business with him for eight years. She most often dealt in small amounts. Three days before the terrible event, however, she took out a large amount in gold. One of the men in the office carried the money home for her.

Adolphe Le Bon, working at the bank, reports that on the day in question, he went with Madame L. to her home with two bags of gold. When the door opened, Mademoiselle L. appeared and took one of the bags; the old lady took the other. He left soon after that. There was no one in the street at the time. It is a side street, where you are not likely to see many people.

William Bird, tailor, states that he was one of those who entered the house. He is an Englishman who has lived in Paris for two years. He was one of the first to go up the stairs and hear the angry voices. The low voice was a Frenchman. He could make out a number of words, but can remember only "What the devil!" and "My God!" Then there was the sound of people fighting—the quick, dry sound of feet moving quickly across the floor. The high voice was very loud, much louder than the low voice. He is sure it was not the voice of an Englishman. It appeared to be that of a German, and may have been a woman's. But he doesn't know German.

Four of these people were called back for more questioning. Aside from what they had already said, they added that the windows in the room were closed and locked from within. Every inch of the house was gone over in the most careful manner. Long brushes were pushed up the chimney to see if anything was there. The time between hearing the voices and entering the room was from three to five minutes. Some people said more, some less. They all agreed that the door was difficult to open.

Alfonzo Garcio, undertaker, lives on the Rue Morgue, and is from Spain. He entered the house with the others, but he did not go up the stairs. His nerves are very weak, and he did not want to become excited. He heard the voices. One was a Frenchman, and the other was English, he is sure. He doesn't know English well, but he can tell, he says, by the rise and fall in tone.

Alberto Montani, who makes cakes and such, states that he was one of the first to go up the stairs. The low voice was French, judging from several words he heard. The voice seemed to be ordering, or asking, the other person to do something. The high voice, he couldn't understand. It was quick and not even. He thinks it must be Russian, though he has never spoken to a Russian before. He is Italian himself.

Everyone agrees that there is no way out the back of the house. So no one could have escaped without being noticed by the people coming up the stairs. It took four or five men to get Mademoiselle L.'s body down from the chimney. It was not easy work.

Paul Dumas, doctor, was called to the scene of the terrible event early the next morning. Both bodies were now in the room on the fourth floor. The body of the daughter was in a sad state, with many cuts on it. No doubt, they were due to the fact that she had been pushed up inside the chimney. There were many black and blue marks around the neck area. They were made, it seemed, by human fingers. The face had turned a strange color, and the eyes stood out from the head. In Dr. Dumas's opinion, Mademoiselle L. had been choked to death.

According to Dr. Dumas, the condition of the mother's body was even more terrible. Many of the woman's bones were broken. The whole body was a chain of black and blue marks. It was impossible to say how this had been done. Perhaps it was done with a heavy piece of wood or iron, or maybe a chair, but only in the hands of a very strong man. No woman was strong enough to do such a thing. The head had been separated from the body by a very sharp object.

Although several other people were questioned, nothing new came to light. This must be the first case of its kind in the history of Paris. Nothing seems to make sense, and no one has any idea how it happened. The police have not done their work well this time. Not a single good idea has been presented by any party.

The evening paper stated that St. Roch quarter was still in an excited state. The house had been gone over again, and more people had been questioned. But nothing new had come of it. The

THE BEST SHORT STORIES OF EDGAR ALLAN POE

paper did say, however, that Adolphe Le Bon was being held by the police. No reason was given for this, other than what was already known.

Dupin seemed very interested in the case, although he said nothing about it. After he heard that Le Bon was being held by the police, however, he asked my opinion for the first time.

I said that I had to agree with all of Paris in believing it impossible to say who the murderer was.

"It is hard to tell what happened from the information we have now," Dupin replied. "The Paris police are often said to be clever, but the fact is that they have no method. They just do what comes to mind at the moment. They get results from hard work, not from thought. They may find one or two important facts, but they work too hard on these facts and lose sight of the big picture. It is the same with stars. You can see them better if you look a little to one side, not directly at them.

"As for this case, let's take a look at the scene

of the crime before we form an opinion. It should be fun."

I thought it a little strange to use the word "fun" about this case, but I didn't say anything.

"Le Bon did me a favor once," Dupin continued. "This is my chance to return it."

We arrived at Madame L.'s house in the evening. There were a number of people standing outside, looking up at the closed windows. We walked down the street and then around to the back of the house. Dupin looked closely not only at the house in question but at all the houses around it. I could not understand why Dupin should be so interested in the neighboring houses.

We returned to the front of the house and were let in by the police. We went up to the fourth floor. There we saw the bodies of Madame L. and her daughter. The room was in the same shocking condition. I saw nothing different from what had appeared in the paper. Dupin studied everything closely, including the two bodies. We then went to look at the other rooms and at the yard in back. By the time we had finished, it had grown quite dark outside. On the way home, Dupin stopped by the office of one of the daily papers.

He said nothing about the case until noon the next day, when he suddenly asked if I had seen anything strange about the house.

"No, nothing special," I replied. "At least, nothing more than appeared in the paper."

"I think we need not worry ourselves about what appeared in the paper," Dupin said. "Let's consider the police, however. First, they cannot understand *why* the killings were so terrible in nature. Second, they don't know *how* voices could be heard but no one was seen leaving the building. They cannot understand other facts either, such as the state of the room, the body in the chimney, and the condition of Madame L.'s body. The police's powers of reasoning seem to have come to a complete stop. They appear to have made the common mistake of confusing what is *not usual* with what cannot be understood. The question the police should ask themselves is not 'What has happened here?' but 'What has happened here that has never happened before?' The reason I know what happened is because it is so difficult to understand."

I could only look at him with my mouth open, completely at a loss for words.

"I am now waiting for a person who may not be the killer but who at least played some part in the murders. I expect that he is not responsible for the terrible way in which the killings were carried out. But we must be prepared in case he is. Here are two pistols. We will use them if we must."

I took one of the pistols. When Dupin spoke again, he spoke as if to himself. Although he faced the wall, his eyes seemed to see something else.

"The voices were not those of the women themselves. There is no doubt about that. But in the interviews there was something strange. Didn't you notice anything strange?"

I replied that all agreed that the low voice was a Frenchman, but they couldn't agree on the high voice.

"Yes, that is what they said," he continued. "But is there not something strange about that? A Frenchman, a German, a Spaniard, an Englishman, and a Dutchman—all think that the voice belongs to someone from a different country. Here I would like to point out three things. First, one person thought the strange voice to be harsh rather than high. Second, others said the voice was quick and not even in sound. Third, no one could make out a single word spoken by the high voice.

"All this leads me to understand this case in a certain way. Or I should say that I now understand this case in the only way it can be understood. I will not now tell you what that is. But I can say that this understanding caused me to look at the house in a special way.

"Let's once again put ourselves in that terrible room. What do we look for first? We look to see how the murderers got away. Let us consider each of the possible means of escape. First, the police have shown that there are no secret doors in the house. Second, the door to the room in question was locked from the inside. Third, the chimney is not large enough for a human to pass through it. That leaves us with the windows.

"If the murderers had escaped through a front window, they would have been seen by the crowd in the street. They must, therefore, have escaped through a back window. There are two back windows. Not only were they both locked, but a large nail had been driven into the windows to hold them in place. The police tried to open both of them, but could not. They did not think it necessary to take out the nails and then try to open the windows. I, however, looked at the windows with a little more care. I knew that what seemed impossible must be possible.

"I began with the fact that the murderers *must*

have escaped through one of the back windows. But the windows were locked from the inside, which the murderers could not do once they had escaped. *Therefore*, the windows must be able to lock themselves.

"I went to the first window, removed the nail, and tried to open it. The window would not move. There must, I thought, be a spring for opening and closing the window. And feeling around with my hand, I soon discovered it. I pressed the spring and saw that it worked. But I left it at that; I did not raise the window.

"I then put the nail back and thought: someone escaping through this window could have closed it from the outside, and the spring would have locked the window. But the nail could not have been put back where it belonged. If this was true, then the murderers *must* have escaped through the other window. And if the springs of the two windows were the same, then the nails *must* be different. I looked at the spring of the other window and found it to be the same.

I looked at the nail, and it also appeared to be the same. It had been driven deep into the wood. The head of the nail rested firmly inside the nail hole. It was, in fact, the head of the nail that kept the window from being opened.

"You may now think that I had come to the end of the road and could go no further. But if you think that, you have not understood my way of thinking. I had made no mistake in my reasoning. My chain of thought was in no way wrong. Everything led to one thing—the nail.

"I reached out and took hold of the head of the nail. When I pulled on it, it came off in my hand. The rest of the nail was still in the hole. The head appeared to have broken off some time ago. But since it rested firmly in the hole, it had not fallen to the floor. I pressed the spring, and the window rose a few inches; the head of the nail rose with it. Then I closed the window, and the head of the nail moved back into place. The nail *looked* all right, but in fact it could no longer keep the window closed because the head of the nail was not doing its job.

"What had been impossible to understand was now possible. After the murderer had escaped, the window closed because of the spring. The police thought the window would not open because of the nail. But it was not the nail that kept the window closed; it was the spring. They didn't think it necessary to look into the matter any further.

"The next question is how someone could get into the room. As we walked around the house, I noticed a lightning rod about one and a half meters from the window. It would be quite possible for someone to climb up the rod, but the window would still be too far away to enter. However, I then noticed large shutters outside the windows. If these shutters were open, the distance between them and the rod would be about a half meter. The police did not notice this, it seems, because they no longer thought the windows important. If, however, the window was open, a very strong person could climb the rod, jump to the shutter, and then enter the house through the window.

"You must keep in mind that this could only be done by a very strong person. But it *is* possible.

"You may say that what is possible is not necessarily true. That is the way the law would look at it, but it is not my way. My way is that of reason, not law. Now consider these two points:

first, the great strength needed to enter the window, and second, the fact that no one could tell what language the person with the high voice was speaking."

At this point I felt that I was close to understanding what Dupin meant. Close, but not close enough. Dupin continued.

"Now let's take a look at the condition of the room, and try to understand *why* these killings took place. The police seem to think that some clothes were taken, and that could be a motive for the killings. But there were still some very good clothes left in the room. Why weren't those taken? And if clothes were taken, why weren't the two bags of gold taken? Good clothes were not taken; gold was not taken. So these two were not the motive.

"So now we have three points to consider: strange voice, great strength, and no motive. Now let us look at the nature of the crime. A woman is killed in a way that requires great strength and is pushed up a chimney in a way that cannot be called human. There is also the matter of Madame L.'s hair. It had been torn from her head and still retained pieces of skin. It is difficult enough to pull out twenty hairs at the same time, but this was more like half a million, and it was very thick hair as well.

"And then there is the matter of Madame L.'s head being severed from her body. And this was done with nothing more than a razor. I will not go into the question of the black and blue marks on Madame L.'s body. The police say they were made with a heavy piece of wood or iron. I say they were made when the old lady was thrown from the window. But, of course, the police think that the windows could not be opened.

"When we add all of this up, we have someone who is far beyond what we usually consider human. What, then, do you make of it?"

I felt my body go cold as Dupin asked me the question. I replied, "It must be a madman. Someone who has escaped from an institution."

"Perhaps it is natural that you should think like that," Dupin said. "But the voice of such a person would still indicate the language spoken by him or those around him. Even if he could not speak words clearly, he would still have a certain tone of voice. But even if you were right, it would not explain *this*. I found it in Madame L.'s hand. What do you make of it?"

Dupin held out a bit of hair. "Dupin," I said, "this is not . . . this is not hair from a human head."

"I didn't say it was," Dupin replied. "But before we go into that question, look at this drawing I have made. It shows the black and blue marks on Mademoiselle L.'s neck. Especially it shows the marks made by the fingers of the murderer."

Dupin spread the paper out on the table.

"Now try," he said, "to place your fingers exactly over those on the drawing."

I tried to do as I was told, but it was impossible. My fingers would not fit over those on the paper.

"Maybe we should try something else," Dupin continued. "The paper is flat, but the human neck is round. Let's wrap the paper around a piece of wood and try again."

I attempted once again to place my fingers over the marks on the drawing, but it was clear that it could not be done. "This," I said, "is not the mark of a human hand."

"Now, read this page from Cuvier," Dupin said.

The page in question was about a large orangutan in the East Indies. The animal was said to be very strong, wild by nature, and able to imitate the actions of human beings. I understood at once what this meant.

"The hand in Cuvier is the same as in your drawing. There is no mistake about it. And the hair you found in Madame L.'s hand is also the same. But still, I do not understand. There were two voices, and one of them was a Frenchman's."

"True," said Dupin. "And you will remember that the Frenchman was trying to get the other party to do something.

"It is possible, or even likely, that the Frenchman had nothing to do with the killings. The orangutan may have escaped him. The man may have followed the orangutan to the house, but the excited animal would not allow himself to be taken home. In fact, the animal is still at large. You may say that I am guessing here. And since it is difficult to explain my thinking to another, let's call it guessing. However, if the Frenchman had nothing to do with the murders, then this notice I put in the paper should bring him to this house."

He handed me a newspaper often read by sailors. It read as follows:

Caught

A large orangutan was caught early in the morning in the Bois de Boulogne. The owner (who is a sailor on a Maltese ship) may pick up the animal by coming to the following address (address given).

"How do you know who the man is?" I asked him.

"I do not *know* it. I am not *sure* of it," Dupin replied. "But I found this ribbon in the yard behind the house. It is the type worn by sailors. And it is tied in a special way found in Malta. It is not the type of thing that either Madame L. or her daughter would wear.

"If I am wrong about the man being on a Maltese ship, he will only think that I have made a mistake. If I am right, however, then he will think that I know who he is. And if he does not come to pick up the orangutan, it will seem as if he is afraid of something, which he wouldn't want.

"You will notice that, according to the paper, the animal was caught in the Bois de Boulogne, which is a great distance from the Rue Morgue. The man will think that no one will tie the orangutan to the killings. If that is the case, he will think it better to pick up the animal and keep it until the whole matter blows over. After that, he can sell the orangutan for a good price."

At this point we heard a noise outside.

"Be ready," Dupin said. "Don't show your pistol until I give the sign."

We heard someone coming up the stairs. Then the person stopped. And then he started coming up again. Dupin moved to the door. When the man had reached the door, Dupin quickly opened it and said, "Come in."

Judging from the man's clothes, he was a sailor. His face was dark from being out in the sun a lot. He was carrying a large cudgel.

"Sit down, my friend," Dupin said. "I suppose you have come for the orangutan. It is a fine animal, and I suppose very valuable. How old is he?"

The man suddenly looked as if a great weight had being lifted from his shoulders. He said, "I have no way of knowing. He must not be more than five or six years old. Do you have him here?"

"No, not here," Dupin replied. "We don't have the space. You can get him in the morning. Are you prepared to show that the animal is indeed yours?"

"Yes, I am," the man replied.

"I shall be sorry to part with him," Dupin said.

"I don't expect you to go to all this trouble for nothing," the man said. "I am willing to pay any amount within reason."

"Well," replied Dupin, "that is very fair. Let me see. What do I want in return? How about you telling me everything you know about the killings on the Rue Morgue?"

Dupin said these last words in a low, quiet voice. Just as quietly he walked to the door and locked it. He then sat down, taking a pistol from his coat pocket and slowly placing it on the table.

The man suddenly turned red in the face and took hold of his cudgel. He started to stand up, but then thought better of it. His face had now turned white, and he looked like death warmed over. He said nothing, and I couldn't help feeling sorry for him.

"My friend," Dupin said, "don't worry yourself too much. We do not mean to hurt you in any way. I promise on my honor. I know that you are innocent in the matter of the Rue Morgue. But you did play a part, however small. I cannot explain how I know all this, but I do. As a man of honor, you must tell me all you know. Another person is being held by the police as the murderer."

"So help me God," the man said, "I will tell you all I know, but I don't expect you to believe half of what I say. Still, I will come clean, even if I have to die for it."

In short, what the man said was this. Not long ago he and a friend were traveling in Borneo. It is there that they caught the orangutan. His friend died not long after that, and so the orangutan became his. It hadn't been easy to get the animal back to Paris because of its wild nature. In Paris he kept it in a room where no one would see it. The animal had hurt its foot on the ship. As soon as it got better, the man planned to sell it.

Early one morning, coming home from a drinking party, the man discovered that the orangutan had escaped from its own room and was now in his room. The animal had a razor in its hand and was trying to shave its face. It had seen the man doing this before, and was trying to do the same.

The man knew how dangerous a razor could be in the hands of a wild animal. For a moment he was at a loss what to do. Then he remembered his whip. He had used it before to keep the animal quiet. But this time, as soon as the orangutan saw the whip, it rushed out of the room, jumped through a window, and ran out into the street.

The man followed as fast as he could. The orangutan, still holding the razor, would sometimes stop and look back. But when the man got close, it would turn and run on ahead. This continued for quite some time. The streets were dark and empty. It was almost three in the morning.

When the orangutan came to the Rue Morgue, it looked up and saw a light coming from the fourth floor of a house. Then it spotted the lightning rod and started to climb it. It still had the razor in one hand. At the top, it reached over to take hold of a shutter and then went through a window into the house. The man tried to follow. But at the top of the rod, he could not reach the shutter. The most he could do was look inside through the window. What he saw made his blood run cold.

It was exactly at this moment that the women's cries tore the night air. It seems that the women had been looking at some papers on the floor. They were sitting with their backs to the window. When they heard the shutter move, they thought it was the wind. They did not realize that an orangutan was standing right behind them.

As the man watched, the animal took Madame L. by the hair and waved the razor in front of her face, as if to give her a shave. The daughter lay on the floor. She had passed out from shock. Perhaps, at first, the animal had not meant to hurt Madame L. But when she fought against him, and when her cries grew louder as he pulled the hair from her head, the animal lost control of himself. With one quick movement of the razor, he cut the old lady's head from her body.

The sight of blood made the animal even wilder. He threw himself on the body of the daughter. With his fingers on her neck, he pressed down with all his strength until she no longer moved. He stood, looked around, and saw the dead face of Madame L. looking toward him. Then he seemed to remember the whip and his fear of the whip. Now he was afraid. He ran around the room, picking things up and throwing them about. He seemed to realize that he must put the bodies in a place where they would not be found. This is when he picked up the daughter and pushed her up the chimney. The old lady he threw out the window.

When the animal carried the old lady's body to the window, the man cried out. His cries and the terrible sounds of the orangutan were the voices heard by the people coming up the stairs. The man quickly went down the rod and left the scene as fast as he could. His first thought was no longer for the orangutan, but for his own safety.

There is little more to say. The orangutan must have escaped through the window, closing it by chance on his way out.

In the end, the man found the animal and sold it for a good price. Le Bon was freed by the police when Dupin told them the whole story.

The police were not happy that Dupin had solved the case and not them. They said that he should mind his own business. But Dupin had no hard feelings. He said, "Let them talk, if it makes them feel better. They are not bad people. I especially like the way they carefully study things that are not, in fact, real, and how they say, 'Impossible!' to what is right before their eyes."

The Black Cat

幼い頃から動物好きだった私は、若くして結婚後、同じように動物好きな妻と共にさまざまな動物を購入して飼っていた。中でもプルートーという名の黒猫は私によくなついていた。しかし、次第に酒におぼれるようになった私は、不機嫌に駆られて飼っている動物を虐待するようになっていった。

読みはじめる前に

　The Black Cat で使われている用語です。わからない語は
巻末のワードリストで確認しましょう。

☐ ax	☐ establish	☐ monk
☐ brick	☐ excessive	☐ outburst
☐ chief	☐ faithful	☐ perversity
☐ claim	☐ fury	☐ plaster
☐ comparison	☐ gallows	☐ principal
☐ confident	☐ hangman	☐ projection
☐ deny	☐ hatred	☐ rub
☐ desire	☐ hung	☐ struggle
☐ downfall	☐ mad	☐ underwent

登場人物・用語解説

I 私　この物語の語り手。優しく動物好きだったが、酒におぼれ
るようになり、性格が変わってしまう。あまのじゃくな一面
を持つ。

wife 妻　私の動物好きを知り、いろいろなペットを買ってくる。

Pluto プルートー　私のお気に入りの飼いネコ。全身が真っ黒で、
語り手によくなついている。

cat ネコ　ある晩酒場で私に拾われる。プルートーにそっくりだ
が、胸のあたりだけ白い。

**a man formed in the image of God 神の像に似せて造られた
人間**　旧約聖書の「創世記」には、神は天地創造の際に、自
分の姿をかたどって人間を造り出したと書かれている。

THE BLACK CAT

I don't expect you to believe the wild story I am about to tell. If I did, it would only show that I am truly mad. The truth is, I hardly believe the story myself. Yet I am not mad, and I don't think I am dreaming. Tomorrow I must die, so today I want to tell the story and ease my mind. My goal is to place before the world a series of everyday events, as simply and plainly as I can. In the end, these events planted fear in my heart, filled my mind with pain, and destroyed me completely. But I will not try to explain away the events. To me, they have brought nothing but terror; to others, however, they may just seem strange, nothing more. Perhaps someday, some clever person will find a simple, logical explanation for these events. Perhaps someday, these terrible events will be seen as nothing but the result of very natural causes and effects.

Since childhood, I was known to be a quiet,

kind child. I had such a tender heart that other children often made fun of me. I especially liked animals. My parents were very good to me in this respect and gave me a number of pets. I spent a great deal of time with these animals, and I was especially happy when feeding or petting them. This aspect of my personality became stronger as I grew older, and as an adult I found that it was my principal source of pleasure in life. Anyone who has kept a dog knows how wise and faithful they can be, how much pleasure they give to their owners. Animals can be so heart-warming that they make human beings look bad by comparison.

I married early, and my wife's character was not unlike my own. Seeing how much I liked animals, she lost no time in buying some very nice pets. We had birds, fish, a fine dog, rabbits, a small monkey, and a *cat*.

The cat was a large, beautiful animal, entirely black. It was quite intelligent. Looking at the cat, my wife would sometimes mention the old

THE BLACK CAT

idea that black cats were, in reality, witches. She wasn't serious when she said this, however. I mention it now only because I happen to remember it.

Pluto—this was the cat's name—was my favorite pet and friend. I was the one who fed him, and he always followed me around the house. I had a hard time keeping him from following me through the streets.

Our friendship lasted for several years. However, during that time my character underwent a huge change. I hate to admit it, but this change was due to excessive drinking. Day by day I became more difficult to live with. Day by day I grew less concerned for the feelings of others. I spoke to my wife in ways I shouldn't have. I even allowed myself to strike her. My pets also came to feel the difference in me. Not only did I stop paying attention to them, I also treated them badly. Pluto, however, I still cared for, or cared for enough not to raise a hand against him. But the other animals were not so lucky. As my drinking problem grew more serious, I began to treat even old Pluto badly.

One night, I returned home after drinking entirely too much. I had the feeling that the cat was avoiding me. I angrily picked it up. Afraid, the cat bit me on the hand. The fury of a devil took control of me. I was no longer myself. My original self seemed to have flown away. It was replaced by a drunk, excited, unknown creature. I took a small knife from my pocket. I took hold of the cat by the neck. Lifting the knife, I cut out one of its eyes. Thinking about it now, I feel less than human.

When I had slept off all the wine of the night before, I returned to reason. I felt terrible about what I had done. I felt sorry for my crime. But the feeling was not strong enough to change my character for the better. I soon returned to wine to forget it all.

With the passing of time, the cat slowly got better. One eye looked absolutely terrible, but it no longer seemed to cause any pain. He went about the house as usual, but as might be expected, he kept a good distance between us. My old self felt sorry that the cat now hated me. But this feeling soon gave way to one of anger. Then this anger gave way to perversity—the desire to do what is not to one's benefit. No one understands this, not wise men, not professors, not doctors. But I am absolutely certain that perversity is one of the oldest, most important, and chief feelings of the human mind. Who has not done something for the simple reason that they knew they should not? Who has not broken the law for the simple reason that they knew they shouldn't?

It was this perversity that would lead to my final downfall. It was the desire to cause harm to my own self for no good reason. It was this that drove me to do wrong to the cat once again. One morning, in cold blood, I put a rope around its neck and hung it from a tree. I did it with tears streaming from my eyes, with sadness in my heart. I hung it from the tree because I knew that it had once loved me. I knew that it had done me no wrong. It was I that was doing wrong. I knew that. I knew that God in Heaven would not close his eyes to what I had done.

On the night that I had done the criminal act, I was awoken by the cry of "Fire!" The covers on my bed had caught fire. The whole house was filled with smoke. With difficulty, I, my wife, and the servant managed to escape. The house was completely destroyed. Everything I owned in the world had gone up in smoke. My whole future looked as black as the night around me.

I am not so weak as to try to establish a relationship of cause and effect between the killing of the cat and the fire. But since I am dealing with a chain of events, I don't wish to leave any fact out of the picture. On the day after the fire, I visited what was left of the house. All the walls, except one, had fallen in. The only wall that had not been destroyed was in the middle of the house. It was, in fact, the wall against which the head of my bed had rested. Around the wall a number of people had gathered. They were carefully examining a part of the wall and saying, "Strange!" "How odd!" I went closer and looked where they were pointing. There, on the wall, was the picture of a huge cat. The picture was very correct and detailed. Surprisingly so, in fact. There was a rope around the animal's neck.

When I first laid eyes on this "wonder"—for you can imagine nothing more unexpected—I was filled with feelings that cannot be described. But shortly, reason came to my aid. The cat, I remembered, had been hung in the tree just outside my window. When the cry of "Fire!" went up, the garden had quickly filled with a crowd of people. Some person in the crowd must have cut the cat down and thrown it through the window into my room. That person was probably trying to wake me up. The other walls must have fallen against the cat and pressed it into the wall behind my bed. The body of the cat had disappeared in the fire, but its outer form had been left on the wall.

Thus my reason helped me to explain this very strange sight. But my heart was not entirely satisfied, and it would not let go of the picture of the cat on the wall. For months this picture stayed with me. I almost came to feel—but not

The Black Cat

quite—sorry for what I had done. In the places where I often went to drink, I began to look around for a similar cat to replace the lost one.

One night, half out of my mind, I sat in a particularly terrible bar. Across the room, I noticed a black object, sitting on an old chair. I was surprised, because I had been looking at this chair for some time, and I had not noticed the object until now. It was a black cat, a very large one. It was as large as Pluto, in fact. And it looked very much like Pluto except for one thing. Pluto was entirely black, but this cat had a large white area covering the front of its body. When I went up and touched it, it rose and rubbed against my hand. It seemed to be happy that I had taken notice of it. This, then, was the cat I was looking for. I offered to buy it from the owner of the bar, but he claimed to know nothing about it, to have never seen it before.

I continued to pet the cat, and when I was ready to go, it appeared to want to come along. I allowed it to follow me, reaching down now and then to pet it. When we reached the house, it came in and made itself at home. My wife quickly took a liking to it.

For my part, however, I soon found it impossible to continue to like the animal. This was quite the opposite of what I had expected. Why did I feel this way? I am not sure. Perhaps because it was so clear that it liked me. Slowly the feeling of dislike turned into hatred. I began to avoid the cat. At first my memories of Pluto prevented me from raising a hand against the cat. But as my feelings against it became stronger and stronger, I avoided it as if it were the source of some terrible disease.

My feelings against the cat increased, no doubt, when I discovered the next day that it had also lost an eye. This only made my wife love it more. She was still full of the loving feelings that I myself once had, feelings that were once the source of my simplest and purest pleasures.

The more I hated the cat, however, the more it seemed to like me. It followed me around so closely—it kept so near my side—that the reader will have difficulty imagining it. When I sat, it would lie at my feet or climb up on my lap. If I stood up, it would get between my feet and nearly throw me down. At times I longed to kill it with a blow, but I didn't. This was partly because of my memory of my former crime, and partly—to tell the truth—because I was so afraid of the animal.

It was not that I feared physical harm from the cat. Even now, as I write this from prison, I can only say that my deep feelings against the cat came from something that may seem of no importance at all. My wife had mentioned the white hair on the cat several times. This was the only difference between it and Pluto. The mark didn't have a clear shape at the beginning, but little by little it called to mind the shape of a certain object. My mind struggled to deny what it saw. My mouth refused to say its name. For this reason alone, I would have destroyed the cat. If I had dared. But the terrible form could no longer be denied. It was the picture of a GALLOWS. Oh, crime! Oh, pain! Oh, death!

Now I felt lower than any human being. The lowest of the low. And it was an animal, an animal the same as the one I had killed . . . It was just such an animal that had brought me down. Me, a man formed in the image of God! Now I knew no rest, either by day or by night. During the day, the animal never left me alone. During the night, I would wake from terrible dreams. The cat would be lying on my chest, its breath falling on my face. I could not shake it off. I could not shake off the heavy weight on my heart.

Weighed down like this, all good left me. Evil thoughts were my only friends. The darkest and lowest of thoughts. My mind turned to hatred of all things, of all human beings. I gave myself up to wild emotions, to outbursts that were beyond my control. My wife was the one who had to suffer, my patient wife.

One day she came down with me into the

basement of the old house in which we lived. The cat followed at my feet and nearly threw me down the stairs. This drove me to the edge of madness. I quickly picked up an ax and lifted it above my head. I was ready to aim a blow at the cat, which would have killed it instantly. But my wife reached out and stopped me. This drove me beyond the edge of madness. I removed her hand and drove the ax into her brain. She fell dead without a sound.

Without a moment's delay, I began to think of how to hide the body. I knew that I couldn't take it out of the house without being seen by the neighbors. Many possibilities entered my mind. I thought of cutting up the body into small pieces and burning them in the fire, of digging a grave in the floor of the basement and burying the body there, of throwing it down the well in the yard, of putting the body into a box and mailing it off as a regular package. Finally, I had an idea that was better than all the rest. I would wall up the body in the basement. I had heard that monks did this to their enemies in the middle ages.

The basement seemed perfectly suited to this plan. The walls were not well built, and the plaster had not hardened because of the dampness in the air. In one spot there was a projection that perhaps had formerly been a fireplace, but had later been filled in. I was sure that I could remove the bricks, put in the body, and then wall it up again. No one would be able to tell the difference. It turned out that I was right. I did everything according to plan, and when I had finished, I was happy with the results. "Here at last," I said to myself, "everything has been perfectly done."

The next step was to find the animal that had been the cause of all this. I had decided to put it to death. And if I had found it just then, that is exactly what I would have done. But perhaps because of the anger I had displayed earlier, the cat had wisely chosen to stay out of my way. You cannot imagine what a relief this was to me. The cat didn't appear that night either. Thus for the first night since the cat had come to live with us, I slept as soundly as a baby, though I was a murderer.

A second and third day passed, but still no sign of the cat. I now felt free, entirely free. The cat was gone, never to be seen again. My happiness cannot be described! Any guilt I felt was of little importance. Some questions had been asked, but they were easily answered. A search had been made, but of course nothing had been discovered. My future looked bright, very bright indeed.

On the fourth day after the murder, the police appeared unexpectedly and carried out another search of the house. I was not terribly concerned, however, since I was completely confident of how I had hid the body. The officers asked me to stay with them while they searched. They looked high and low, missing nothing. Finally, for the third or fourth time, they went down to the basement. I was as calm as calm can be. My

THE BEST SHORT STORIES OF EDGAR ALLAN POE

heart didn't miss a single beat. I walked calmly up and down. I looked as though I had not a care in the world. The police finally finished and were ready to leave. I felt so happy that I had to say something. I burned to say just one word, as a sign of my victory.

"Gentlemen," I said at last, as they went up the stairs. "I hope you are completely satisfied now, and that you have no more doubts about the house. By the way, gentlemen, this . . . this is a very well-built house." Wanting very much to say something, I hardly knew what I was saying. "Yes, well-built, I say. These walls . . . Are you going, gentlemen? These walls . . . " And from a kind of madness, with my walking stick I struck the wall behind which my wife was hidden.

Oh, may the gods deliver me from the devil of darkness! As the sound of my walking stick sank into silence, it was answered by a voice from the walled grave. It was a cry, at first low and broken, like the crying of a child. Then it grew into one long, loud, and continuing scream. There was

58

nothing human about it. A voice filled with fear, but also with victory. A cry from hell, issuing from the mouths of both the damned and the devils.

I cannot hope to describe my own thoughts at this development. A weakness overcame me, and I fell against the facing wall. For a moment the officers on the stairs didn't move. They seemed frozen by the sound of the cry. In the next moment, a dozen strong arms were tearing at the wall, which came down in one piece. My wife had suffered greatly in appearance since I last saw her. But she was standing straight up, facing the officers. On her head sat the terrible animal! Its red mouth open, fire coming from its one eye. The animal that had caused me to become a murderer, the animal that would now deliver me to the hangman! I had walled it up with the body of my wife!

The Gold Bug

私が数週間ぶりにサリバン島で隠遁生活を送る友人
ウィリアム・ルグランのもとを訪れると、彼は新種
の黄金虫を発見したと言って興奮の最中にいた。1
カ月後、私のもとにルグランの召使ジュピターが訪
ねてきた。彼の話では、ルグランはあの日から様子
がすっかりおかしくなってしまたという。

読みはじめる前に

The Gold Bug で使われている用語です。わからない語は
巻末のワードリストで確認しましょう。

☐ antennae	☐ insane	☐ scythe
☐ code	☐ melancholy	☐ skull
☐ diameter	☐ misanthropy	☐ spade
☐ dig	☐ myrtle	☐ specimen
☐ enthusiasm	☐ parchment	☐ stream
☐ hut	☐ scarab	☐ trunk

用語解説

Sullivan's Island サリヴァン島　物語の舞台となるサウスカロ
　ライナ州チャールストン湾にある島。

Fort Moultrie モールトリー要塞　サリヴァン島にある要塞。こ
　こに立てこもりイギリス軍を防いだモールトリー大佐にち
　なんで名づけられた。

Huguenot ユグノー　16、17 世紀頃のフランスの新教徒。

Captain Kidd キャプテン・キッド　実在したスコットランド生
　まれの海賊船船長。もとは海賊退治も行う私掠船の船長だ
　ったが、やがて海賊となり、1701 年ロンドンで絞首刑となる。
　世界のどこかに財宝を埋めたという伝説がある。

主な登場人物

I 私　この物語の語り手。チャールストン在住で、ときおりルグ
　ランを訪ねる。

William Legrand ウィリアム・ルグラン　私の友人。非常に頭が
　よく教養があるが、人間嫌いですぐに何かに熱中したりふさ
　ぎ込んだりする。貝殻や虫の収集が趣味。

Jupiter ジュピター　ルグランの召使。年老いた黒人で、ルグラ
　ンを "Master Will（ウィル旦那）" と呼んで慕う。

Lieutenant G_____ G_____中尉　ルグランの知り合い。ル
　グランの発見した黄金虫を貸してほしいと頼む。

THE GOLD BUG

Many years ago I became friends with a Mr. William Legrand. He came from an old Huguenot family and had once been wealthy, but a series of unlucky events had left him poor. He left the home of his fathers, New Orleans, and moved to Sullivan's Island, near Charleston, South Carolina. This island is a very unusual one. It is made up of little more than sand, and is three miles long and no more than a quarter of a mile wide. It is separated from the mainland by a small, slow-moving stream. At the west end, there is Fort Moultrie and some sad-looking buildings, which are rented out to visitors from Charleston during the summer. Aside from the west end and the line of white beach on the seacoast, the rest is covered by a thick growth of myrtle, which reaches a height of fifteen or twenty feet and fills the air with its smell.

In this growth of myrtle, not far from the

eastern end of the island, was Legrand's hut. It was here that, by accident, I first came to know him. This soon grew into friendship, for Legrand was a very interesting person. He was well educated and had a powerful mind. On the other hand, he had more than a touch of misanthropy, and he was subject to fits of enthusiasm and melancholy. He had a great many books, but he did little reading. He spent most of his time fishing or hunting, or walking along the beach and through the myrtle, looking for shells or bugs. His collection of bugs would have made even the greatest collector proud.

On his walks, Legrand was usually followed by an old black man called Jupiter. Jupiter had been freed by the Legrand family before it met with money troubles, but he was determined to continue to look after his "Master Will." It may well be that the family had planted that idea in his head, thinking that Legrand did, indeed, need some looking after.

The winters on Sullivan's Island are not very

The Gold Bug

cold, and it is not often that you need a fire. About the middle of October 18__, however, there was one day that was quite cold. Just before the sun went down, I was hurrying through the myrtle to my friend's place. I hadn't visited for several weeks. I was living in Charleston at the time, and the means of transportation then were not what they are today. I knocked on the door, and when no one answered, I found the key in the usual place and let myself in. A nice fire was already going. That was quite unusual, and I was happy to see it. I took off my coat, sat in a chair by the fire, and waited patiently for Legrand and Jupiter to return.

Soon after dark they arrived and gave me a warm welcome. Jupiter, smiling from ear to ear, hurried to prepare something to eat. Legrand was in one of his fits of enthusiasm. He had found an unusual shell, and, more than that, he had caught a scarab beetle that he believed to be totally new. He said that he would like to have my opinion tomorrow morning.

"Why not tonight?" I asked, warming my hands by the fire.

"If I had only known that you were here!" said Legrand. "But it's been quite a while since I saw you, and how could I know that you would visit tonight? As I was coming home, I met Lieutenant G____, from the fort, and I lent him the bug. So it'll be impossible for you to see it until tomorrow. Stay the night, and I'll send Jupiter down for it as the sun is coming up. It is the loveliest thing you ever saw!"

"What? The sun?"

"Not the sun! The bug, of course. It's the color of pure gold and about the size of a hickory nut. It has two black spots near one end, and another larger one at the other end. It has these antennae . . . "

"He's all gold, Master Will. I keep telling you," said Jupiter. "It's a gold bug, every bit of it, inside and out, except for the wings. Never felt a bug so heavy in my life."

"Well, I suppose it is all gold, Jupiter," said

Legrand very seriously. "But that's no reason to let the food burn, is it?" Then, turning to me, he said, "The color is almost enough to make you believe, like Jupiter, that it's made of gold. I have never seen such color—but, of course, you can see for yourself tomorrow. Right now, though, I can give you an idea of the shape." He sat at a small table, where there was a pen and ink but no paper. He looked for some in a drawer, but found none.

"Never mind," he said at last, "this will do." He pulled from his coat pocket a dirty piece of paper and started to draw on it. While he was doing that, I sat by the fire, trying to warm my body. When he had finished the drawing, he handed it to me without rising. As I took the paper, I heard a bark outside the door. Jupiter opened it, and Legrand's large Newfoundland came rushing in and jumped on me. We had become good friends during my previous visits. Having petted the dog a little, I turned my attention to the paper. To tell the truth, I wasn't sure what he had drawn.

"Well," I said after a few minutes. "This is a strange scarab, I must say. It's new to me. I've never seen anything like it before. It looks more like a skull or a death's head than anything I have ever seen."

"A death's head!" repeated Legrand. "Oh, yes, it does look like that on paper, doesn't it. The two spots at the top look like eyes, right. And

the longer one at the bottom looks like a mouth. And the overall shape is oval."

"Yes, maybe," I said. "But I'm afraid that you're not much of an artist. I think I'll have to see the real thing before I can say anything more."

"Well, I don't know," he said a little unhappily. "I draw alright. Or I should, anyway. I've had good teachers. And I don't think I'm completely stupid."

"But, Legrand, you must be playing with me then," I said. "This is a very good skull. In fact, it's an excellent skull. But your scarab must be very strange if it looks like this. And I don't see the antennae you spoke of."

"What?" said Legrand, who seemed to be getting somewhat excited. "You must be able to see them. I drew them just as they are on the bug."

"Well, well, maybe you have," I said, handing him the drawing without another word. I didn't want to excite him any more than he was already.

But there were certainly no antennae there, and the whole thing did look very much like a skull.

He took the paper and was about to throw it into the fire when something caught his attention. All at once his face grew terribly red, and then just as suddenly, perfectly white. For a while he sat looking at the drawing. Then he went to the other side of the room, sat on a box, and studied the drawing some more, turning it this way and that. He didn't say anything, and I thought it best not to ask him anything. Finally he put the drawing into a drawer and locked it.

He then seemed to recover himself, though he didn't return to the subject of the scarab with the same warmth of feeling. He appeared normal, but his thoughts seemed to be elsewhere. As the evening wore on, he was less and less quick to reply to anything I said. I had planned to spend the night, as I had done before. But given his state of mind, I decided to leave. He didn't try to stop me, but he sent me off in a much more friendly manner than usual.

THE GOLD BUG

It was about a month after this—during which time I had seen nothing of Legrand—when his man Jupiter came to visit me in Charleston. I had never seen him look so down in the mouth. I was afraid that something serious had happened to my friend.

"Well, Jupiter," I said. "What's the matter now? How's your master?"

"Well, to tell the truth, he's not as well as he might be."

"Not well! I'm sorry to hear that. What's the matter?"

"Well, that's it! He doesn't complain of anything. But still, he's very sick."

"Very sick, Jupiter! Why didn't you say so? Is he in bed?"

"No, he's not in bed. But still, I'm very, very worried about Master Will."

"Jupiter, I don't understand. You say your master is sick. Hasn't he told you what the problem is?"

"Well, Master, don't you go and get excited,

too! If you ask him, Master Will will just say there's nothing wrong with him. But if that's true, what makes him go out and look around this way and that, his head down, his shoulders up, and looking white as a goose? And he keeps ciphering all the time."

"Keeps doing what, Jupiter?"

"Keeps working with figures. The strangest figures I ever saw. I'm so afraid of what's going to happen. I have to keep a close eye on him all the time. The other day he slipped out before the sun was up and was gone all day long. I had a big stick ready to give him a beating when he got home, but then I couldn't do it when I saw how poorly he looked."

"Eh? Oh, yes, I think you shouldn't be too hard on him, Jupiter. Don't give him a beating. I don't think he could stand that. But don't you have any idea what brought on this illness? Has anything unpleasant happened since I last saw you?"

"No, Master, nothing since then. I think it was

before then. Exactly on the day you were there, in fact."

"How? What do you mean?"

"Why, Master, I mean the bug, that's what."

"The what?"

"The bug. I'm certain that Master Will has been bitten somewhere on his head by that gold bug."

"And why would you think that, Jupiter?"

"Because of its claws, and its mouth. I've never seen a bug like that. It kicks and bites anything that comes near it. Master Will caught it first, but he had to let go of it mighty quick. That's when he was bitten, I think. I didn't like the look of the bug's mouth, so I didn't try to pick it up with my fingers. I used some paper, and wrapped it up in that. Put some paper in its mouth, too. That was the way to do it."

"And you think that your master was actually bitten by the bug, and that's what made him sick?"

"I don't *think*. I know. What makes him

73

dream about gold so much if he wasn't bitten by the gold bug? I've heard about those gold bugs before this."

"But how do you know he dreams about gold?"

"How do I know? Because he talks about it in his dreams. That's how."

"Well, Jupiter, maybe you're right. But to what do I owe the honor of this visit?"

"The honor, Master?"

"Did you bring a message from Mr. Legrand?"

"No, but I brought this note."

Here Jupiter handed me the following note:

My Dear _____:

Why haven't I seen you for so long? I hope that I haven't hurt your feelings in some way, but I doubt that is the case. Since I last saw you, I have not been feeling myself. I have something important I would like to tell you. However, I am not sure how to tell it, or if I should, in fact, tell it at all.

THE GOLD BUG

I haven't been well for some time now, and Jupiter causes me more trouble by kindly trying to take care of me. Would you believe it? The other day he was prepared to teach me a lesson with a stick because I had slipped out and spent the day among the hills on the mainland. The only thing that saved me from a beating was how poorly I looked.

If at all possible, I would like to see you come back with Jupiter. *Do* come. I would like to see you *tonight* on important business. I assure you it is a matter of the *highest* importance.

Ever Yours,
William Legrand

I made up my mind at once to go and see him. When we were ready to get in the boat for the island, I noticed a scythe and three spades in the bottom of the boat.

"What is the meaning of this, Jupiter?" I asked.

"That's a scythe and spades, Master."

"Very true, but what are they doing here?"

"Well, Master Will insisted that I buy them in town, though I didn't have much money."

"But what in the name of God is Master Will going to do with them?"

"That's more than I know, and let the devil take me if he knows himself. It's all because of that bug."

Finding that I wasn't going to learn much more from Jupiter, whose mind seemed totally occupied by the bug, I stepped into the boat and we made sail. With a strong wind, we soon landed north of Fort Moultrie, and from there walked to Legrand's place. It was about three in the afternoon when we arrived. Legrand gave me a warm welcome and weakly shook my hand. His face was so white that one could only think he was sick. His eyes shone strangely. After asking about his health, I had no choice but to ask if he had gotten the scarab back from Lieutenant G____.

"Oh, yes," he replied, turning a bright red. "I got it from him the next morning. Nothing could make me part with that scarab. You know, Jupiter is absolutely right about it."

"In what way?" I asked, fearing what his answer might be.

"In guessing that the bug is made of real gold," he said, absolutely serious. I hoped that the shock I felt didn't show on my face.

"This bug is going to make me rich," he continued with a happy smile. "It's going to help me recover all that my family lost. Is it any wonder, then, that I prize it? Now that I have been so lucky as to get it, all I have to do is use it properly to get to where the gold is. Jupiter, bring me the scarab!"

"What, the bug, Master? I'd rather not trouble the bug. You'd better get it yourself." Hearing this, Legrand rose in the most serious manner and brought back the bug in a glass case. It was a beautiful specimen, unknown to science at that time. From that point of view, it was very valuable. And it did seem to be covered in shiny gold. And it was surprisingly heavy. Considering everything, I wasn't surprised about Jupiter's opinion concerning the bug, but I couldn't, for the life of me, understand how Legrand could agree with it.

"I sent for you . . . ," he said seriously, when I had finished examining the beetle. "I sent for you to ask your advice and help in regard to the scarab."

"Legrand, my friend," I said, interrupting him. "You are clearly unwell. You have to take care of your health. You must go to bed, and I'll stay a few days to look after you. You have a fever and . . . "

"Feel my pulse," he said.

I felt it, and it seemed normal.

"But you may be sick without a fever. You should do what I say just this once. First, go to bed. Second . . . "

"You're wrong," he said, stopping me. "I'm as well as can be expected, considering how excited

I am. If you want to help me, you should help me return to normal."

"And how can I do that?"

"Very easily. Jupiter and I are going on a little outing into the hills on the mainland. We need the help of a third party, and you are the only person we can trust. Whether we succeed or not, I'm sure I'll come back here in a much better frame of mind."

"I'm happy to help you out in any way," I replied. "But you don't mean to say that this devilish beetle has something to do with the outing?"

"It does."

"Then, I'm afraid I'll have to excuse myself."

"I'm sorry to hear that. Very sorry. I guess we'll have to do it on our own."

"Do it on your own? You must be mad! But wait. How long do you plan to be gone?"

"Probably all night. We'll leave right away and be back by the time the sun is up, at the latest."

"And will you promise that once this

craziness is over, and this bug business is settled once and for all, you will follow my advice as your doctor, without question?"

"I promise. Now let's be off. We have no time to lose."

With a heavy heart I followed my friend. We started about four o'clock—Legrand, Jupiter, the dog, and myself. Jupiter insisted on carrying the scythe and spades, more from the fear of putting them in the hands of his master than anything else. Jupiter looked very dogged, and the only words that escaped his lips were, "That devil of a bug!" For my part, I took charge of a couple of lanterns, while Legrand had the scarab on the end of a string, which he swung back and forth. Watching Legrand and his strange ways, I couldn't keep tears from filling my eyes. For the moment, however, I thought it best to let him be, and wait for a better chance to influence him. While walking, I tried to find out what the purpose of the outing was, but the most I could get from Legrand was, "We shall see."

THE GOLD BUG

We crossed the stream at the head of the island and went on to some wild-looking land on the other side, where it seemed that no human being had ever set foot. Legrand led the way, a determined look on his face. He stopped only now and then to check some marks on the ground that he had apparently left on a previous occasion.

We went on like this for about two hours. The sun was just setting when we reached a region that seemed less friendly to human beings than any we had seen so far. It was a kind of table-land, and above it rose the peak of a hill, covered with thick vegetation and huge rocks. The rocks rested against trees, which was the only thing that prevented them from plunging into the many narrow valleys that lay below.

The table itself was covered with low, thick vegetation, and it would have been impossible to force our way through it if we had not had the scythe. Following Legrand's directions, Jupiter proceeded to clear a way from where we were

THE BEST SHORT STORIES OF EDGAR ALLAN POE

to the foot of a very tall tulip tree. This tree—in its form, its wonderful leaves, the spread of its branches, and the general dignity of its appearance—was far grander than any tree I had ever seen. When we reached the tree, Legrand turned to Jupiter and asked if he thought he could climb it. Jupiter seemed surprised by the question and for a few moments didn't reply. Finally he walked around the tree, looking at it closely, and said:

"Yes, Master, there is no tree I can't climb."

"Then, up you go," said Legrand. "It'll soon be too dark to see anything."

"How far up, Master Will?" Jupiter wanted to know.

"Get up the main trunk first, then I'll tell you which way to go. And here, take the beetle with you."

"The bug, Master, the gold bug!" cried Jupiter, drawing back. "Why would I do that? Let the devil take me if I do."

"Why, Jupiter, a big fellow like you, afraid of a dead beetle! You can carry it up by this string.

If you don't, I'll be forced to hit you on the head with this spade."

"What're you talking about, Master? You're always trying to make trouble for poor old Jupiter. I was only having a little fun with you. Me, afraid of a bug? Why should I be afraid of a bug?" Taking hold of one end of the string and holding the bug as far from his body as possible, Jupiter started to climb the tree. Before long, he had climbed up to the first main branch, some sixty or seventy feet above the ground.

"What should I do now, Master Will?" Jupiter asked.

"Keep going up the largest branch, the one on this side," Legrand told him. Jupiter did as he was told, going higher and higher, until he could no longer be seen among the leaves. Shortly his voice was heard calling down.

"How much further, Master Will?"

"How high are you now?" asked Legrand.

"Pretty high. I can see the sky through the top of the tree."

"Never mind the sky. Just listen to what I say. Look down and count the big branches below you. How many are there?"

"One, two, three, four, five. I've gone past five so far, on this side."

"Then climb up one more."

In a few minutes Jupiter called out again, saying that he was now on the seventh branch.

"Now, Jupiter," said Legrand in an excited voice. "I want you to work your way out on that branch as far as you can go. If you see anything strange, let me know." At this point, I finally had to admit that my friend's state of mind was far from normal. I had to admit, in fact, that he was insane. I began to think how I could get him home. While I was running this question through my mind, I heard Jupiter's voice again.

"Don't think I want to go out on this branch much further. It's dead almost all the way to the end."

"Did you say it was a dead branch, Jupiter?" cried Legrand in an odd voice.

The Gold Bug

"Yes, Sir. Dead as dead can be. Gone to meet its Maker. Yes, Sir."

"What in heaven's name should I do?" asked Legrand, talking to himself.

"Do?" I said. "Come home with me and go to bed. Come now, let's go. It's getting late, and remember your promise."

"Jupiter," called out Legrand, paying no attention to me whatsoever. "Do you hear me?"

"Yes, Master. Clear as a bell."

"Try cutting the wood with your knife. See how rotten it is."

"It's rotten, Master. Sure enough," replied Jupiter in a few minutes. "It's not as bad as it might be, though. By myself, I could go out a little further."

"'By yourself?' What do you mean?"

"Why, I mean the bug, Master. It's a very heavy bug. Suppose I drop the bug down first. The branch could carry me by myself, for sure."

"Why, you fool!" Legrand seemed happy that it wasn't anything more serious. "You're just full

85

of hot air. You drop that beetle and I'll break your neck. Now, listen. Do you hear me?"

"Yes, Sir. I hear you. There's no need to shout."

"Well, listen now. You go out on the branch as far as it's safe, without letting go of the bug. If you do that, I'll give you a silver dollar as soon as you get down, right on the spot."

"I'm going, Master Will. I'm going," replied Jupiter. "Almost out to the end now."

"Out to the end!" cried Legrand. "Did you say you were out to the end?"

"I'm getting there, Master. Ooooh, Lord above, what is this here?"

"Well," Legrand cried with delight. "What is it?"

"Why, it's nothing but a skull. Somebody's left their head up in the tree and the birds have eaten every bit of meat off it."

"A skull, you say? Very good. Now, how is it fixed to the tree? What holds it on?"

"Alright, Master. Let me look. Why, this is

The Gold Bug

strange as strange can be. There's a big nail in the skull holding it to the tree."

"Now, Jupiter. Do exactly what I tell you. Do you hear me?"

"Yes, Sir. I hear you."

"Pay attention, then! Find the left eye of the skull."

"Hum. Hah. Now that's strange. There's no left eye at all."

"Damn you! Do you know your right hand from your left?"

"Yes, I know that. I know all about that. It's my left hand that I chop wood with."

"That's right. You're left-handed. And your left eye is on the same side as your left hand. Now, I suppose you can find the left eye of the skull, or the place where the left eye was. Have you found it?"

For several moments, there was no answer. And then Jupiter asked, "Is the left eye of the skull on the same side as the left hand of the skull? Because the skull doesn't have any left hand at all. Never mind! I've got the left eye now. Here it is, the left eye. Now what do I do with it?"

"Let the bug drop through it, as far as the string will reach. But be careful not to let go of the string."

THE GOLD BUG

"All that's done, Master Will. It was pretty easy to put the bug through the hole. Watch for it there below."

While the two were talking, Jupiter couldn't be seen up in the tree. But the bug, which he had let drop down, could now be seen hanging from the end of the string. It was shining like a large drop of gold in the last rays of the sun. The scarab hung clear of any branches and, if allowed to fall, would have fallen right at our feet. Legrand picked up the scythe and cleared a space just below the bug. Having finished, he told Jupiter to let go of the string and come down from the tree.

After Legrand had driven a short stick into the ground exactly where the bug had fallen, he produced a tape measure from his pocket. He fixed one end of the tape to the tree, pulled it around the short stick, and then stretched out the tape fifty feet and drove another stick into the ground. Around this stick he drew a circle about four feet in diameter. Then, taking one

89

spade himself and giving one each to me and Jupiter, Legrand asked us to start digging as fast as we could.

To tell the truth, digging had never been one of my favorite activities, and I wanted very much to decline the offer. The night was coming on, and I was already tired from so much walking. But if I did refuse to help, I wasn't sure how Legrand would react. With Jupiter's aid, I could, of course, take Legrand home by force. But I doubted that Jupiter would help me out in any way if it came down to a difference of opinion between Jupiter's master and myself.

I had no doubt that Legrand's mind was under the influence of the old Southern stories about buried treasure, and that this influence had been strengthened by the finding of the scarab and perhaps by Jupiter's insistence that the bug was made of gold. There was also the fact that Legrand somehow thought the bug was going to help him recover all that his family had lost in the past. In the end, I decided that the best

THE GOLD BUG

course was to get the digging done as quickly as possible and show Legrand that he was mistaken in all his crazy ideas about the bug.

We lit the lanterns and fell to work, though I couldn't help wishing that it was for a more sensible cause. We must have appeared quite a strange group, digging away in the darkness of the night under the weak light of a lantern.

We dug without stop for two hours. The only difficulty we met with was the barking of the dog, who was quite interested in our activities. The dog grew so noisy that Legrand began to worry that its barking might attract the attention of someone passing through the area. Of course, I would have been quite happy to have a visitor. However, Legrand was of a different opinion, and the dog was dealt with by Jupiter, who tied its mouth shut.

After two hours we had reached a depth of five feet, but still there was no sign of any buried money. All work stopped for a moment, and I hoped that this would mark the end of the whole foolish undertaking. Legrand, however, began again, this time digging deeper and widening the circle. Still, nothing appeared. Finally Legrand stopped and came out of the hole—deep, sad lines written large on his face. I truly felt sorry for him. He put on his coat, and Jupiter began to gather up the tools. Without a word being exchanged, we turned toward home.

We had taken only a dozen steps or so when Legrand suddenly went up to Jupiter and took hold of him by the shirt. Jupiter opened his eyes and mouth wide and fell to the ground.

"You fool!" shouted Legrand. "Tell me, here and now, which is your left eye."

"My goodness, Master Will! Isn't this my left eye, for certain?" and Jupiter put his hand over his right eye, and kept it there as if to protect it.

"I thought so! Hot dog! I thought so!" Legrand let go of Jupiter and did a little dance. Jupiter got to his feet, looking from his master to me, then from me to his master.

"Come! We have to go back," Legrand said.

THE GOLD BUG

"The game's not over yet." He led the way back to the tree.

"Jupiter," he said. "Was the skull facing away from the branch or in toward it?"

"It was away from the branch, Master Will. So the birds could get at the eyes without any trouble."

Then, touching each of Jupiter's eyes in turn, Legrand said, "Was it this eye you dropped the bug through, or this one?"

"It was this eye. Just as you told me. The left eye!" Here Jupiter touched his right eye.

"That's enough," Legrand said. "We have to do it all over again."

I now saw that while Legrand might be crazy, there was some method in what he was doing. He took the first stick out of the ground and moved it about three inches to the west. Then he got out his tape and measured the distance again. He drove in the second stick about three yards from where the old one had been.

He drew a new circle, somewhat larger than

the one he had drawn before. Again we started digging. I was very tired, but I no longer thought it was a complete waste of time. I'm not sure what caused this change of mind. Somehow or other, I had become interested—no, actually excited. Perhaps it was the thoughtfulness in Legrand's approach, the way he seemed to know what he was doing. Now I dug seriously, stopping once in a while to see if I had uncovered anything.

As such thoughts ran through my mind, an hour and a half went by. This is when the dog started acting up again, making a great deal of noise. There was a difference this time, however. The dog had just been playing the first time, but now it seemed quite serious. When Jupiter tried to get hold of it, it jumped into the hole and started digging. In a few moments it had uncovered some human bones, enough to form two complete skeletons. Using the spade, we dug deeper and discovered three or four gold coins.

At the sight of the coins, Jupiter became

THE GOLD BUG

happy beyond words. His master, however, looked disappointed. He told us to keep working. But hardly were the words out of his mouth when the toe of my shoe caught on an iron ring in the loose earth and I fell forward.

We now worked as hard as we could. Never in my life have I spent such an exciting ten minutes. What our efforts produced was a wooden chest, three and a half feet long, three feet wide, and two and a half feet deep. The whole was strengthened by bands of iron. On each side of the chest, near the top, were three rings of iron—six in all—by means of which six people could lift the box. No matter how hard we tried, however, we were unable to move the chest more than a few inches. As it turned out, the top was easy to remove, which we did. And there, before us, was a treasure of gold and jewels that few men have ever laid eyes on.

It is beyond the power of words to describe my feelings as I looked down at this wonderful sight. Legrand was so excited that he had run

The Best Short Stories of Edgar Allan Poe

out of energy, and spoke very little. Jupiter's face seemed emptied of all feeling. Recovering himself, he jumped into the hole and buried his arms in the gold. For a while, he just left his arms there, as if he were enjoying a hot bath. Then, as if speaking to himself, he said, "And this all comes from the gold bug. That pretty gold bug.

THE GOLD BUG

That poor little gold bug that you treated so bad. Aren't you sorry now, Jupiter, that you treated that bug so bad?"

I finally had to suggest that we should perhaps move the treasure. It was getting late, and we had to get started if we were going to finish before the sun came up. It was difficult to decide exactly what to do next since everyone had his own ideas, and so we spent a good deal of time discussing the matter. What we finally did was remove two-thirds of the contents and lift the chest out of the hole. The coins and other things we laid out on the ground and left the dog to watch over them, with Jupiter's firm orders to the dog that it was not to move from the spot or open its mouth until we returned. We then left with the chest, and after some hard work, got back home at one o'clock in the morning. We were completely worn out, and we couldn't find it in ourselves to do anything more for a while.

We rested until two, had something to eat, and then started back, taking with us three large

97

bags. A little before four we arrived at the site, divided the rest of the treasure as equally as possible among us, and started back again, leaving the hole as it was. We arrived at Legrand's place just as the sun began to rise behind the trees.

We were now entirely burned out, and it was difficult to settle our nerves. After getting a few hours of restless sleep, we all woke up at exactly the same time to take a closer look at what we had found.

The chest had been filled to the top, and we spent all of that day, and the greater part of the next day, in examining its contents, which showed no signs of any planned order or organization. Having gone through it all, we found ourselves in possession of greater riches than expected. In coin alone, there was more than $450,000. As for the jewels, it was more difficult to figure out their value. There were 110 diamonds, 18 rubies, 310 emeralds, 21 sapphires, and an opal. There were also a good many gold objects, including rings, chains, crosses, watches, and one huge bowl. The total value seemed to be around $1,500,000.

After the excitement of the moment had died down somewhat, Legrand could see how much I longed to hear how he had solved the puzzle and knew where to find the treasure. He began with the drawing.

"I suppose you remember the night when I handed you my drawing of the scarab," he said. "You probably also remember that I became quite angry when you said it looked like a death's head. At first I thought you were joking. But later I remembered the strange spots on the back of the bug and admitted to myself that your argument was not entirely wrong. Still, I didn't like your saying that my drawing wasn't very good, for there are some people who think I am quite good. So when you handed back the parchment, I was ready to throw it into the fire."

"You mean the paper, not the parchment," I said.

"No. It looked very much like paper, and

at first that's what I thought it was. But when I started to draw on it, I realized that it was a very thin piece of parchment. Well, just as I was in the act of throwing it away, I saw a death's head exactly where I had drawn the bug. I didn't know what to think. I knew that my drawing was very different in detail, though there did seem to be some general similarity. So I went to the other end of the room and looked at the drawing more closely with a candle. When I turned the parchment over, I saw my drawing on the other side, just as I had made it. At first I just felt surprised that my drawing and the death's head should be the same in outline and location. It seemed very strange, to say the least, that there should be a matching drawing exactly behind my own. For a while, my mind simply stopped working. That seems to be the case when the mind cannot establish a cause and effect relationship. It just comes to a stop.

"But then I received another shock. I remembered that there had been no drawing on either side of the parchment when I made my drawing. I was perfectly certain of that. I clearly remember turning the parchment over several times in search of the cleanest spot to draw. If the skull had been there, I would have noticed it, without fail. This was truly a mystery that I couldn't explain. Yet, even at that point, my mind carried the smallest seed of an idea that would lead us to our great discovery. I put the parchment away and decided not to think about it until I was alone.

"After you had gone, and Jupiter was fast asleep, I decided to look into the matter a little more closely. First I considered how I had gotten the parchment in the first place. The spot where we discovered the scarab was on the coast of the mainland, a little above the high water mark. The bug bit me when I picked it up, and I dropped it. The bug flew toward Jupiter, and he began looking for a leaf or something to pick it up with. That's when both of us, about the same time, saw the piece of parchment, which we thought was paper. A corner was sticking out of the sand. Nearby I noticed what looked like the wreckage of a longboat. It must have been quite old because it had broken apart and now looked nothing like a boat at all.

"Well, Jupiter picked up the bug, wrapped it in the parchment, and gave it to me. On the way home, we ran into Lieutenant G____. I showed him the bug, and he asked if he could keep it one night to study it. When I agreed, he stuck it quickly into his pocket, without the parchment. Perhaps he thought I might change my mind, so he wanted to take the bug and leave as soon as possible. I was left with the parchment in my hand, and without thinking, I must have put it in my pocket.

"You probably remember when I went to the table to make the drawing. I looked in the drawer for some paper but found none. I then searched in my pockets, thinking I might find an old letter there. That's when my hand fell on the parchment. I'm telling you all this in such detail because later it became very important.

"In fact, I had already established a kind of connection, though you may wonder how I could do it so quickly. First, there was an old boat lying along the coast; second, there was a piece of parchment in the sand near it. So how are these two tied together? The answer is that the skull, or death's head, is the mark of a pirate ship, as everyone knows. It's on the flag they raise when attacking another ship.

"The fact that what we have is parchment, not paper, is also quite important. Paper is usually used for things that are not of lasting importance because paper is easy to write on. Parchment, on the other hand, lasts a long time and therefore is suited to something you wish to preserve. This suggests that the death's head had some special meaning."

"But the big question is," I said, "how did the death's head get on the parchment if it wasn't there when you drew the scarab?"

"That question, Sir," said Legrand, "lies at the heart of the matter. I didn't draw it, and you didn't draw it, and yet it is there. I tried to remember every move that was made after I gave you the drawing. It was cold, so you were sitting close to the fire. Just as you had received the parchment and were about to look at it, the door opened and the Newfoundland came in and jumped on you. With your left hand, you petted the dog, and with your right hand you held the parchment away from you, in the direction of the fire. I was about to warn you about the parchment catching fire when you let the dog go and started looking at the drawing. Thinking about this, I realized that it must have been the heat that brought out the drawing of the skull. As you know, there are certain chemical preparations used in writing that are visible only when exposed to heat. When the material cools, the writing can no longer be seen, but it appears once more if the material is heated again.

"Examining the death's head once again, I noticed that some lines were clearer than others. I thought that, perhaps, the heat had not been equally applied. I started a fire and heated the parchment as equally as I could. I then found that, diagonally opposite the spot where the death's head was, there was another drawing. At first I thought it was a goat, but looking closer, I was sure it was a kid, or a young goat."

"Whether it was a goat or a kid, I don't really see the difference," I said.

"Well, there is in fact quite a difference," Legrand replied. "I suppose you have heard of Captain Kidd, the pirate. I take the drawing of a kid to be his signature, so to speak. I say signature because of its position and from the fact that I expected to find some writing between it and the skull."

"And you believed the treasure," I said, "to have been buried by Captain Kidd."

"Why, yes, as a matter of fact. There has always been talk about money having been buried along the coast by Kidd and his men. If Kidd hadn't buried any treasure, or had buried some but had dug it up later, then I don't believe there would be so much talk about the subject. But the fact that there *is* talk is due, I believe, to Kidd's having buried some treasure but being prevented from digging it later up by some unexpected event, such as the loss of the parchment. His men, I assume, knew about this and were the ones who spread the talk about the lost treasure. I was certain that the parchment had something to do with the whole matter."

"So, what did you do next?" I asked.

"Since the parchment had been in the sand for a long while, and was not in what you would call good condition, I decided to clean it up by running warm water over it. I then applied heat to the parchment a number of times. In the process, the following lines appeared:

53‡‡†305))6*;4826)4‡.)4‡);806*;48†8¶60))85;
1‡(;:‡*8†83(88)5*†;46(;88*96*?;8)*‡(;485);5*†
2:*‡(;4956*;(?*7)8¶8*;42(5*—485);)6†8)4‡‡;1(
‡9;48081;8:8‡1;48†85;4)485†528806*81(‡9;4
8;(88;4(‡?34;48)4‡;161;:188;‡?;

THE GOLD BUG

"Well," I said, "this is not much help to me. I'm as much in the dark as ever."

"Obviously, it's a message in code," Legrand went on. "And from what we know of Captain Kidd, I didn't expect it would be a very difficult one. A simple sailor who had the key would have to be able to solve it."

"And you solved it without the key?"

"Yes, I did. And quite easily, too. I've worked on codes much more difficult than this one. It takes a certain type of mind, which I seem to have.

"The first question is the language of the message. Since, looking at the drawing, I could see that there is a play on the English words "Kidd" and "kid," I assumed that the language would be English. Once that was decided, the next step was to count the letters in the message to see which are the most frequently used. This table shows the results:

character		number of times in message	
8	=	33	
;	=	27	
4	=	19	
‡,)	=	16	each
*	=	14	
5	=	12	
(	=	11	
6	=	10	
†,1	=	8	each
0	=	5	
9,3,2,?,:	=	4	each
¶	=	2	
—,7,.	=	1	each

"Now, in English, the most frequently used letter is *e*. After *e*, the order is *a o i d h n r s t u y c f g l m w b k p q x z*. All in all, there is hardly an English sentence in which *e* is not by far the most common letter.

"Now, in the table I made, the most common letter is '8,' so we can assume that '8' is the letter *e*. Since *e* is often doubled in English words (as in *speed* or *seen*), we can check the message to see if '8' is doubled, and we find that it happens five times.

"Next, we know that *the* is one of the most common words in the English language, and that it, of course, ends with an *e*. So we look at the message for a combination of three letters ending in '8' that appears frequently. What we find is that the combination ';48' is repeated seven times. So we can assume that ';' equals *t*; '4' equals *h*; and, of course, '8' equals *e*. This represents a big step forward.

"Now that we have three letters, we can see if these three letters form the beginnings or endings of other words. For example, near the end of the fourth line in the message we find ';48,' which we know equals *the*. After that, we see ';(88,' which can be written as 't(ee.' Going through the English alphabet, we find that the only letter that can possibly be equal to '(' is *r*, giving us 'tree.' So now we have another letter to work with, that is, '(' equals *r*.

"Working in this way, we are at last able to represent ten of the most important letters, as follows:

5	represents	a
†	represents	d
8	represents	e
3	represents	g
4	represents	h
6	represents	i
*	represents	n
‡	represents	o
(	represents	r
;	represents	t
?	represents	u

"I believe you get the general idea, and there is no need to go further. Now is the right time, I think, to give you a full translation of the message, which I have punctuated for easier reading."

A good glass in the Bishop's hostel in the Devil's seat—forty-one degrees and thirteen minutes—northeast and by north—main trunk seventh branch east side—shoot from the left eye of the death's-head—a bee line from the tree through the shot fifty feet out.

"I'm afraid that this doesn't mean much to me," I said. "I'm still in the dark."

"For a few days," Legrand replied, "it left me in the dark, too. During that time, I checked around Sullivan's Island to see if anyone had heard of Bishop's hostel or Bishop's hotel. It turned out that no one had. Then it occurred to me that 'Bishop' might be a misspelling for 'Bessop,' which was an old name in the area. So I went over to the Bessop farm and asked the oldest person there if she had ever heard of Bessop's hotel. She said that, no, she hadn't, but she did know of a place called Bessop's Castle, which wasn't, in fact, a castle but a high rock. She led me there, and as I looked at the rock, I discovered that there was one place that looked very much like a seat or chair. This must, I thought, be the 'Devil's seat' mentioned in the message.

"As for the 'good glass' mentioned in the message, I was sure that meant a telescope. This is the usual meaning of 'glass' among sailors. So the message must mean that one should use a telescope while sitting in the Devil's seat. And 'forty-one degrees and thirteen minutes' and 'northeast and by north' were intended to be the directions in which to point the glass. I left for home at once to get a telescope and came back to the rock as quickly as I could.

"Sitting myself in the Devil's seat, I found that I could face in only one direction. I aimed the telescope in the direction given in the message, and I noticed at once an opening in the woods some distance away, where one tree stood out above all the rest. I also noticed a white spot, and I adjusted the telescope so that I could get a closer look. What I saw was a human skull.

"At this point, I more or less considered the mystery solved. The words 'main trunk, seventh branch, east side' could only refer to the position of the skull on the tree. 'Shoot from the left eye of the Death's head' must mean to drop a bullet from the left eye of the skull. 'Bee-line,' of course, means a straight line. And all the rest fell into place."

"All this," I said, "seems very clear, indeed. What did you do after you left the rock?"

"I started to go home. But at once I noticed that the tree with the skull could only be seen from the Devil's seat. Once you left that spot, you no longer knew where the tree was. So the next morning, getting up before Jupiter, I went in search of the tree. After a good deal of difficulty, I found it. The rest of the story, you know as well as I do."

"There is only one thing that puzzles me.

What are we to make of the skeletons that we found in the hole?"

"I can't answer that question any better than you can. However, we might think of it in this way. If Captain Kidd did bury the treasure—and I have no doubt that he did—he must have had help. Once the work had been finished, Kidd may have decided to do away with the two men, so that he would be the only one who knew the secret. Perhaps a couple of blows with a spade is all that was needed; or maybe it took a dozen blows. Who can tell?"

Word List

- 本文で使われている全ての語を掲載しています（LEVEL 1、2）。ただし、LEVEL 3 以上は、中学校レベルの語を含みません。
- 語形が規則変化する語の見出しは原形で示しています。不規則変化語は本文中で使われている形になっています。
- 一般的な意味を紹介していますので、一部の語で本文で実際に使われている品詞や意味と合っていないことがあります。
- 品詞は以下のように示しています。

名 名詞	代 代名詞	形 形容詞	副 副詞	動 動詞	助 助動詞
前 前置詞	接 接続詞	間 間投詞	冠 冠詞	略 略語	俗 俗語
頭 接頭語	尾 接尾語	記 記号	関 関係代名詞		

A

☐ **about** 熟 be about to まさに～しようとしている、～するところだ

☐ **absolutely** 副 ①完全に、確実に ②《yesを強調する返事として》そうですとも

☐ **accident** 名 ①(不慮の) 事故、災難 ②偶然 by accident 偶然に

☐ **according** 副《 – to ～》～によれば[よると]、～に従って

☐ **act** 名 行為、行い 動 ①行動する ②機能する ③演じる act up 暴れる

☐ **activity** 名 活動、活気

☐ **actually** 副 実際に、本当に、実は

☐ **add** 動 ①加える、足す ②足し算をする ③言い添える

☐ **address** 名 ①住所、アドレス ②演説 動 ①あて名を書く ②演説をする、話しかける

☐ **adjust** 動 ①適応する[させる]、慣れる ②調整する

☐ **admit** 動 認める、許可する、入れる

☐ **Adolphe Le Bon** 名 アドルフ・ル・ボン《人名》

☐ **adult** 名 大人、成人 形 大人の、成人した

☐ **advice** 名 忠告、助言、意見

☐ **against** 前 ①～に対して、～に反対して、(規則など)に違反して ②～にもたれて

☐ **age** 名 ①年齢 ②時代、年代

☐ **aid** 名 援助(者)、助け come to one's aid ～に援助の手を差し伸べる 動 援助する、助ける、手伝う

☐ **aim** 動 ①(武器・カメラなどを) 向ける ②ねらう、目指す 名 ねらい、目標

☐ **Alberto Montani** 名 アルベルト・モンタニ《人名》

☐ **Alfonzo Garcio** 名 アルフォンゾ・ガルシオ《人名》

☐ **all** 熟 all at once 突然、出し抜けに all day long 一日中、終日 all in all 全体から見て all over ～中で、全体に亘って、～の至る所で、全て終わって、もうだめで all right 大丈夫で、よろしい、申し分ない、わかった、承知した all the time ずっと、いつも、その間ずっと all the way through 始めから終わりまで、完全に in all 全部で not ～ at all 少しも[全然]～ない once and for all これを最後にきっぱりと

☐ **allow** 動 許す、《 – … to ～》…が～するのを可能にする、…に～させて

WORD LIST

おく ②与える

□ **alphabet** 名①アルファベット, 文字, 文字体系 ②初歩

□ **alright** 副よろしい, 申し分ない(= all right)

□ **although** 接〜だけれども, 〜にもかかわらず, たとえ〜でも

□ **amount** 名①量, 額《the –》合計 動《総計〜に》なる

□ **Amsterdam** 名アムステルダム《オランダの首都》

□ **anger** 名怒り 動怒る, 〜を怒らせる

□ **angrily** 副怒って, 腹立たしげに

□ **answer** 動①答える, 応じる ②《– for 〜》〜の責任を負う 名答え, 応答, 返事

□ **antennae** 名antenna (アンテナ・触角) の複数

□ **anyone** 代①《疑問文・条件節で》誰か ②《否定文で》誰も (〜ない) ③《肯定文で》誰でも

□ **anyway** 副①いずれにせよ, ともかく ②どんな方法でも

□ **apart** 副①ばらばらに, 離れて ②別にして, それだけで

□ **apparently** 副見たところ〜らしい, 明らかに

□ **appear** 動①現れる, 見えてくる ②《〜のように》見える, 〜らしい **appear to** するように見える

□ **appearance** 名①現れること, 出現 ②外見, 印象

□ **apply** 動①申し込む, 志願する ②あてはまる ③適用する

□ **approach** 動①接近する ②話を持ちかける 名接近, (〜へ) 近づく道

□ **argument** 名①議論, 論争 ②論拠, 理由

□ **around** 熟**look around** 見回す **look around for** 〜を捜し求める **run around** 走り回る **walk around** 歩き回る, ぶらぶら歩く

□ **article** 名①(法令・誓約などの) 箇条, 項目 ②(新聞・雑誌などの) 記事, 論文

□ **artist** 名芸術家

□ **as** 熟**as a matter of fact** 実際は, 実のところ **as 〜 as ever** 相変わらず, これまでのように **as 〜 as one can** できる限り〜 **as 〜 as possible** できるだけ〜 **as far as** 〜と同じくらい遠く, 〜まで, 〜する限り (では) **as for** 〜に関しては, 〜はどうかと言うと **as if** あたかも〜のように, まるで〜みたいに **as it turned out** 後でわかったことだが **as soon as** 〜するとすぐ, 〜するや否や **as though** あたかも〜のように, まるで〜みたいに **as usual** いつものように, 相変わらず **as well** なお, その上, 同様に **as well as** 〜と同様に **as you know** ご存知のとおり **be seen as** 〜として見られる **just as** (ちょうど) であろうとおり **not so 〜 as** …ほど〜でない **so 〜 as to** ……するほど〜で **such as** たとえば〜, 〜のような

□ **aside** 副わきへ (に), 離れて

□ **asleep** 形眠って (いる状態の) 副眠って, 休止して **fast asleep** ぐっすり眠っている

□ **aspect** 名①状況, 局面, 側面 ②外観, 様子

□ **assume** 動①仮定する, 当然のことと思う ②引き受ける

□ **assure** 動①保障する, 請け負う ②確信をもって言う

□ **attack** 動①襲う, 攻める ②非難する ③(病気が) おかす 名①攻撃, 非難 ②発作, 発病

□ **attempt** 動試みる, 企てる 名試み, 企て, 努力

□ **attention** 名①注意, 集中 ②配慮, 手当て, 世話 **pay attention to** 〜に注意を払う 間《号令として》気をつけ

□ **attract** 動①引きつける, 引く ②魅力がある, 魅了する

117

THE BEST SHORT STORIES OF EDGAR ALLAN POE

☐ **avoid** 動避ける, (～を)しないようにする

☐ **away** 熟do away with ～を捨てる, ～を殺す

☐ **awoken** 動awake (目覚めさせる) の過去分詞

☐ **ax** 名おの 動おので切る

B

☐ **badly** 副①悪く, まずく, へたに ②とても, ひどく

☐ **band** 名ひも, 帯 動①ひもで縛る ②団結する[させる]

☐ **banker** 名銀行家[員]

☐ **bar** 名①酒場 ②棒, かんぬき ③障害(物) 動かんぬきで閉める

☐ **bark** 名①ほえる声, どなり声 ②木の皮 動ほえる, どなる

☐ **basement** 名地下(室), 基部

☐ **beat** 動①打つ, 鼓動する ②打ち負かす 名打つこと, 鼓動, 拍

☐ **beating** 動beat (打つ) の現在分詞 名①打つこと, むち打ち(の罰) ②鼓動 ③敗北

☐ **because of** ～のために, ～の理由で

☐ **bee** 名ミツバチ

☐ **bee-line** 名(巣に戻るミツバチの進路のような) 直線コース

☐ **been** 動be (～である) の過去分詞 動be (～している・～される) の過去分詞

☐ **beetle** 名甲虫, カブトムシ

☐ **behind** 前①～の後ろに, ～の背後に ②～に遅れて, ～に劣って 副①後ろに, 背後に ②遅れて, 劣って

☐ **being** 動bo (＝である) の現在分詞 名存在, 生命, 人間

☐ **believe** 動信じる, 信じている, (～と)思う, 考える

☐ **bell** 名ベル, 鈴, 鐘 動①(ベル・鐘が)鳴る ②ベル[鈴]をつける clear as a bell はっきりと聞こえる

☐ **belong** 動《－to ～》～に属する, ～のものである

☐ **below** 前①～より下に ②～以下の, ～より劣る 副下に[へ]

☐ **benefit** 名利益, 恩恵 動利益を得る, (～の)ためになる

☐ **besides** 前①～に加えて, ～のほかに ②《否定文・疑問文で》～を除いて 副その上, さらに

☐ **Bessop** 名ベソップ《地名》

☐ **Bessop's Castle** ベソップの城

☐ **best** 形最もよい, 最大な[多]の 副最もよく, 最も上手に《the－》①最上のもの ②全力, 精いっぱい

☐ **better** 熟think better of it そうしない方が賢明だと思う

☐ **beyond** 前～を越えて, ～の向こうに 副向こうに

☐ **bishop** 名司教, 主教

☐ **Bishop's hostel** 僧正の宿

☐ **bit** 動bite (かむ) の過去, 過去分詞 名①小片, 少量 ②《a－》少し, ちょっと

☐ **bite** 動かむ, かじる 名かむこと, かみ傷, ひと口

☐ **bitten** 動bite (かむ) の過去分詞

☐ **blood** 名①血, 血液 ②血統, 家柄 ③気質 in cold blood 冷酷に

☐ **blow** 動①(風が)吹く, (風が)～を吹き飛ばす ②息を吹く, (鼻を)かむ ③破裂する 名①(風の)ひと吹き, 突風 ②打撃

☐ **Bois de Boulogne** 名(パリの) ブーローニュの森

☐ **bone** 名①骨, 《-s》骨格 ②《-s》要点, 骨組み 《魚・肉》の骨をとる

☐ **book** 名①本, 書物 ②《the B-》聖書 ③《-s》帳簿 動①記入する, 記帳する ②予約する

☐ **born** 動be born 生まれる 形生ま

WORD LIST

れた, 生まれながらの

- ☐ **Borneo** 名 ボルネオ島
- ☐ **bottom** 名 ①底, 下部, すそ野, ふもと, 最下位, 根底 ②尻 形 底の, 根底の
- ☐ **brain** 名 ①脳 ②知力
- ☐ **branch** 名 ①枝 ②支流, 支部 動 枝を広げる, 枝分かれする
- ☐ **break** 動 ①壊す, 折る ②(記録・法律・約束を)破る ③中断する 名 ①破壊, 割れ目 ②小休止
- ☐ **breath** 名 ①息, 呼吸 ②《a-》(風の)そよぎ, 気配, きざし
- ☐ **brick** 名 レンガ, レンガ状のもの 形 レンガ造りの
- ☐ **bring out** (物)をとりだす, 引き出す, (新製品など)を出す
- ☐ **broken** 動 break (壊す)の過去分詞 形 ①破れた, 壊れた ②落胆した
- ☐ **bug** 名 小虫
- ☐ **building** 動 build (建てる)の現在分詞 名 建物, 建造物, ビルディング
- ☐ **bullet** 名 銃弾, 弾丸状のもの
- ☐ **burn out** 燃え尽きる, 消耗する
- ☐ **burn to do** しきりに〜したがる
- ☐ **bury** 動 ①埋葬する, 埋める ②覆い隠す
- ☐ **business** 名 ①職業, 仕事 ②商売 ③用事 ④出来事, やっかいなこと **mind one's own business** いらぬおせっかいをしない 形 ①職業の ②商売上の

C

- ☐ **C. Auguste Dupin** 名 C・オーギュスト・デュパン《人名》
- ☐ **call** 熟 **call back** 呼び戻す, 折り返し電話する **call out** 叫ぶ, 呼び出す, 声を掛ける
- ☐ **calm** 形 穏やかな, 落ち着いた 名 静けさ, 落ち着き 動 静まる, 静める

- ☐ **calmly** 副 落ち着いて, 静かに
- ☐ **Camille L'Espanaye** 名 カミーユ・レスパネ《人名》
- ☐ **candle** 名 ろうそく
- ☐ **captain** 名 長, 船長, 首領, 主将 動 キャプテン[指揮官]を務める
- ☐ **Captain Kidd** 名 キャプテン・キッド(= William Kidd)(1645–1701)《スコットランドの海賊》
- ☐ **care** 熟 **care for** 〜の世話をする, 〜を扱う, 〜が好きである, 〜を大事に思う **take care of** 〜の世話をする, 〜の面倒を見る, 〜を管理する
- ☐ **carry** 熟 **carry out** 外へ運び出す, [計画を]実行する
- ☐ **case** 名 ①事件, 問題, 事柄 ②実例, 場合 ③実況, 状況, 症状 ④箱 **in case** 〜だといけないので, 万が一〜の場合
- ☐ **catch** 動 ①つかまえる ②追いつく ③(病気に)かかる **catch fire** 火がつく, 引火する **catch on** 〜にぶつける, 〜に引っかかる 名 つかまえること, 捕球
- ☐ **cause** 名 ①原因, 理由, 動機 ②大義, 主張 動 (〜の)原因となる, 引き起こす
- ☐ **certain** 形 ①確実な, 必ず〜する ②(人が)確信した ③ある ④いくらかの 代 (〜の中の)いくつか
- ☐ **certainly** 副 ①確かに, 必ず ②《返答に用いて》もちろん, そのとおり, 承知しました
- ☐ **chain** 名 ①鎖 ②一続き 動 ①鎖でつなぐ ②束縛[拘束]する
- ☐ **chance** 熟 **by chance** 偶然, たまたま
- ☐ **character** 名 ①特性, 個性 ②(小説・劇などの)登場人物 ③文字, 記号 ④品性, 人格
- ☐ **charge** 動 ①(代金を)請求する ②(〜を…に)負わせる ③命じる 名 ①請求金額, 料金 ②責任 ③非難, 告発
- ☐ **Charleston** 名 チャールストン《ア

119

THE BEST SHORT STORIES OF EDGAR ALLAN POE

メリカ, サウスカロライナ州の都市》

□ **check** 動①照合する, 検査する ②阻止［妨害］する ③（所持品を）預ける

□ **chemical** 形化学の, 化学的な 名化学製品［薬品］

□ **chest** 名①大きな箱, 戸棚, たんす ②金庫 ③胸, 肺

□ **chief** 名頭, 長, 親分 形最高位の, 第一の, 主要な

□ **childhood** 名幼年［子ども］時代

□ **children** 名child（子ども）の複数

□ **chimney** 名煙突（状のもの）

□ **choice** 名①選択（の範囲・自由）, えり好み, 選ばれた人［物］ have no choice but to ～するしかない 形精選した

□ **choke** 動①息が詰まる, 窒息する ②つかえる be choked to death 窒息死する 名窒息

□ **chop** 動たたき切る, 切り刻む 名一撃, チョップ, 切り身

□ **cipher** 名①暗号, 暗号文 ②アラビア数字 動①計算する, ～を解く ②～を暗号で書く

□ **circle** 名①円, 円周, 輪 ②循環, 軌道 ③仲間, サークル 動回る, 囲む

□ **claim** 動①主張する ②要求する, 請求する 名①主張, 断言 ②要求, 請求

□ **claw** 名鉤爪 動爪で引っかく

□ **clean** 形①きれいな, 清潔な come clean 白状する ②正当な 動掃除する, よごれを落とす 副①きれいに ②まったく, すっかり

□ **clear** 形①はっきりした, 明白な ②澄んだ ③（よく）晴れた clear as a bell はっきりと聞こえる clear of 離れて 動①はっきりさせる ②片づける ③晴れる 副①はっきりと ②すっかり, 完全に

□ **clearly** 副①明らかに, はっきりと ②《返答に用いて》そのとおり

□ **clever** 形①頭のよい, 利口な ②器用な, 上手な

□ **close** 形①近い ②親しい ③狭い be close to ～に近い 副①接近して ②密集して get close 近づく 動①閉まる, 閉める ②終える, 閉店する

□ **closed** 動close（閉まる）の過去, 過去分詞 形閉じた, 閉鎖した

□ **closely** 副①密接に ②念入りに, 詳しく ③ぴったりと

□ **clothes** 動clothe（服を着せる）の3人称単数現在 名衣服, 身につけるもの

□ **coast** 名海岸, 沿岸 動①滑降する ②（～の）沿岸を航行する ③楽々とやり遂げる

□ **code** 名①法典 ②規準, 慣例 ③コード, 番号 動コード化する

□ **collection** 名収集, 収蔵物

□ **collector** 名集める人, 収集家

□ **combination** 名①結合（状態, 行為）, 団結 ②連合, 同盟

□ **come** 熟come across ～に出くわす, ～に遭遇する come along 一緒に来る, ついて来る come back 戻る come back to ～へ帰ってくる, ～に戻る come clean 白状する come down 下りて来る, 田舎へ来る come down to ～に行き着く come for ～の目的で来る, ～を取りに来る come in 中にはいる, やってくる, 出回る come off 取れる, はずれる come out of ～から出てくる, ～をうまく乗り越える come to light 明らかになる come to pick up ～を取りに来る come to one's aid ～に援助の手を差し伸べる come up 近づいてくる, 浮上する, 水面へ上ってくる

□ **common** 形①共通の, 共同の ②普通の, 平凡な ③一般の, 公共の 名①共有地 ②公園

□ **comparison** 名比較, 対照

□ **complain** 動①不平［苦情］を言う, ぶつぶつ言う ②（病状などを）訴え

120

WORD LIST

る

□ **complete** 形完全な, まったくの, 完成した 動完成させる

□ **completely** 副完全に, すっかり

□ **concerning** 動concern (関係する) の現在分詞 前～についての, 関しての

□ **condition** 名①(健康)状態, 境遇 ②《-s》状況, 様子 ③条件 動適応させる, 条件づける

□ **confident** 形自信のある, 自信に満ちた

□ **confusing** 形混乱させる, 紛らわしい

□ **connection** 名①つながり, 関係 ②縁故

□ **consider** 動①考慮する, ～しようと思う ②(～と)みなす ③気にかける, 思いやる

□ **content** 名①《-s》中身, 内容, 目次 ②満足 形満足して 動満足する[させる]

□ **continue** 動続く, 続ける, (中断後)再開する, (ある方向に)移動していく

□ **control** 動①管理[支配]する ②抑制する, コントロールする 名①管理, 支配(力) ②抑制 **take control of** ～を制御[管理]する, 支配する

□ **correct** 形正しい, 適切な, りっぱな 動(誤りを)訂正する, 直す

□ **could** 助①can (～できる) の過去 ②《控え目な推量・可能性・願望などを表す》

□ **count** 動①数える ②(～を…と)みなす ③重要[大切]である 名計算, 総計, 勘定

□ **couple** 名①2つ, 対 ②夫婦, 一組 ③数個 **a couple of** 2, 3の 動つなぐ, つながる, 関連させる

□ **course** 熟**of course** もちろん, 当然

□ **cover** 動①覆う, 包む, 隠す ②扱う, (～に)わたる, 及ぶ **be covered with** ～でおおわれている 名覆い, カバー

□ **covering** 動cover (覆う) の現在分詞 名覆い 形覆う

□ **craziness** 名狂気

□ **crazy** 形①狂気の, ばかげた, 無茶な ②夢中の, 熱狂的な

□ **creature** 名(神の)創造物, 生物, 動物

□ **crime** 名①(法律上の)罪, 犯罪 ②悪事, よくない行為

□ **criminal** 形犯罪の, 罪深い, 恥ずべき 名犯罪者, 犯人

□ **cross** 動①横切る, 渡る ②じゃまする ③十字を切る 名十字架, 十字形のもの 形不機嫌な

□ **crowd** 動群がる, 混雑する 名群集, 雑踏, 多数, 聴衆

□ **cry** 熟**cry out** 叫ぶ

□ **cudgel** 名こん棒

□ **cut** 熟**cut out** 切り取る, 切り抜く **cut through** ～を切り離す, ～を通り抜ける

□ **Cuvier** 名キュヴィエ (1769–1832) 《フランスの博物学者》

D

□ **daily** 形毎日の, 日常の 副毎日, 日ごとに

□ **damn** 間ちくしょう, くそ《怒り・不満・嫌悪・罵倒》動①だめだと判定する ②けなす, ののしる 副ひどく, まったく

□ **damned** 動damn (だめだと判定する) の過去, 過去分詞 形①非難された, 悪く評された ②ひどい, くそいまいましい 副ひどく, まったく

□ **dampness** 名湿気

□ **dance** 動踊る, ダンスをする 名ダンス, ダンスパーティー

□ **dare** 動《– to ～》思い切って[あえ

THE BEST SHORT STORIES OF EDGAR ALLAN POE

□ **dark** 形①暗い，闇の ②(色が)濃い，(髪が)黒い ③陰うつな 名①《the－》暗がり，闇 ②日暮れ，夜 ③暗い色[影]

□ **darkness** 名暗さ，暗やみ

□ **day** 熟 all day long 一日中，終日 by day 昼間は，日中は day by day 日ごとに one day (過去の)ある日，(未来の)いつか the other day 先日

□ **dead** 形①死んでいる，活気のない，枯れた ②まったくの fall dead 倒れて死ぬ 名《the－》死者たち，故人 副完全に，まったく

□ **deal** 動①分配する ②《－ with [in]～》～を扱う 名①取引，扱い ②(不特定の)量，額 a good [great] deal (of ～) かなり [ずいぶん・大量] (の～)，多額 (の～)

□ **death** 名①死，死ぬこと ②《the－》終えん，消滅 be choked to death 窒息死する to death 死ぬまで，死ぬほど

□ **decline** 動①断る ②傾く ③衰える 名①傾くこと ②下り坂，衰え，衰退

□ **deep** 形①深い，深さ～の ②深遠な ③濃い 副深く

□ **degree** 名①程度，階級，位，身分 ②(温度・角度の)度

□ **delay** 動遅らせる，延期する 名遅延，延期，猶予

□ **delight** 動喜ぶ，喜ばす，楽しむ，楽しませる 名喜び，愉快

□ **deliver** 動①配達する，伝える ②達成する，果たす

□ **deny** 動否定する，断る，受けつけない

□ **depth** 名深さ，奥行き，深いところ

□ **describe** 動 (言葉で)描写する，特色を述べる，説明する

□ **desire** 動強く望む，欲する 名欲望，欲求，願望

□ **destroy** 動破壊する，絶滅させる，無効にする

□ **detail** 名①細部，《-s》詳細 ②《-s》個人情報 動詳しく述べる

□ **determined** 動 determine (決心する)の過去，過去分詞 形決心した，決然とした

□ **development** 名①発達，発展 ②開発

□ **devil** 名①悪魔 (のような人) ②やっかいなこと ③《疑問詞を強調して》いったい全体

□ **devilish** 形①悪魔のような ②のろわしい，極悪な

□ **diagonally** 副対角線上に

□ **diameter** 名直径

□ **diamond** 名①ダイヤモンド ②ひし形

□ **die** 動死ぬ，消滅する die down 弱まる，静まる

□ **difficulty** 名①むずかしさ ②難局，支障，苦情，異議

□ **dig** 動①掘る ②小突く ③探る dig up 掘り起こす，掘り出す 名①突き ②掘ること，発掘

□ **dignity** 名威厳，品位，尊さ，敬意

□ **direction** 名①方向，方角 ②《-s》指示，説明書 ③指導，指揮 in the direction of ～の方向に

□ **directly** 副①じかに ②まっすぐに ③ちょうど

□ **dirty** 形①汚い，汚れた ②卑劣な，不正な 動汚す

□ **disappear** 動見えなくなる，姿を消す，なくなる

□ **discovery** 名発見

□ **discuss** 動議論 [検討] する

□ **disease** 名病気

□ **dislike** 動嫌う 名反感，いや気

□ **display** 動展示する，示す 名展示，陳列，表出

□ **distance** 名距離，隔たり，遠方

122

WORD LIST

□ **divide** 動分かれる, 分ける, 割れる, 割る

□ **do** 熟do away with ～を捨てる, ～を殺す have nothing to do with ～と何の関係もない have no way of doing ～するすべがない, ～しようがない

□ **dog** 名犬

□ **dogged** 形頑固な, 根気強い

□ **double** 形 ①2倍の, 二重の ②対の 副 ①2倍に ②対で 動 ①2倍になる[する] ②兼ねる

□ **doubt** 名 ①疑い, 不確かなこと ②未解決点, 困難 no doubt きっと, おそらく, 確かに there is no doubt (～ということは)疑いない 動疑う

□ **down in the mouth** 落ち込んで

□ **downfall** 名転落, 失墜, 没落, 破滅

□ **dozen** 名1ダース, 12(個)

□ **Dr.** 名～博士,《医者に対して》～先生

□ **draw** 動 ①引く, 引っ張る ②描く ③引き分けになる[する]

□ **drawer** 名 ①引き出し ②ズボン下

□ **drawing** 動draw(引く)の現在分詞 名 ①素描, 製図 ②引くこと

□ **drawn** 動draw(引く)の過去分詞

□ **drew** 動draw(引く)の過去

□ **drink** 動飲む, 飲酒する 名飲み物, 酒, 1杯

□ **drinking** 動drink(飲む)の現在分詞 名飲むこと, 飲酒

□ **drive** 動(人を極端な行動に)走らせる

□ **driven** 動drive(極端な行動に走らせる)の過去分詞

□ **drove** 動drive(極端な行動に走らせる)の過去

□ **drunk** 動drink(飲む)の過去分詞 形(酒に)酔った, 酔いしれた

□ **dry** 形 ①乾燥した ②辛口の 動乾燥する[させる], 干す

□ **due** 形予定された, 期日のきている, 支払われるべき due to ～によって, ～が原因で 名当然の権利

□ **dug** 動dig(掘る)の過去, 過去分詞

□ **Dutchman** 名オランダ人

E

□ **earring** 名《通例-s》イヤリング

□ **ear** 熟smile from ear to ear 満面の笑みを浮かべる

□ **earth** 名 ①《the –》地球 ②大地, 陸地, 土 ③この世

□ **ease** 名安心, 気楽 動安心させる, 楽にする, ゆるめる

□ **easily** 副 ①容易に, たやすく, 苦もなく ②気楽に

□ **East Indies** 《the –》東インド諸島

□ **eastern** 形 ①東方の, 東向きの ②東洋の, 東洋風の

□ **edge** 名 ①刃 ②端, 縁 動 ①刃をつける, 鋭くする ②縁どる, 縁に沿って進む

□ **effect** 名 ①影響, 効果, 結果 ②実施, 発効 動もたらす, 達成する

□ **effort** 名努力(の成果)

□ **eh** 間《略式》えっ(何ですか), もう一度言ってください《驚き・疑いを表したり, 相手に繰り返しを求める》

□ **elsewhere** 副どこかほかの所で[へ]

□ **emerald** 名エメラルド

□ **emotion** 名感激, 感動, 感情

□ **empty** 形 ①空の, 空いている ②(心などが)ぼんやりした, 無意味な 動空になる[する], 注ぐ

□ **end** 熟in the end とうとう, 結局, ついに

□ **enemy** 名敵

THE BEST SHORT STORIES OF EDGAR ALLAN POE

- [ ] **Englishman** 名イングランド人，イギリス人

- [ ] **enough** 形十分な，（〜するに）足る 代十分（な量・数），たくさん 副（〜できる）だけ，十分に，まったく **sure enough** 思ったとおり，確かに

- [ ] **enthusiasm** 名情熱，熱意，熱心

- [ ] **entirely** 副完全に，まったく

- [ ] **equal** 形等しい，均等な，平等な **be equal to** 〜に等しい，〜するだけの能力がある 動匹敵する，等しい 名同等のもの［人］

- [ ] **equally** 副等しく，平等に

- [ ] **escape** 動逃げる，免れる，もれる 名逃亡，脱出，もれ

- [ ] **establish** 動確立する，立証する，設置［設立］する

- [ ] **even** 副①《強意》〜でさえも，〜ですら，いっそう，なおさら ②平等に **even if** たとえ〜でも 形①平らな，水平の ②等しい，均一の ③落ち着いた 動平らになる［する］，釣り合いがとれる

- [ ] **everyday** 形毎日の，日々の

- [ ] **everyone** 代誰でも，皆

- [ ] **everything** 代すべてのこと［もの］，何でも，何もかも

- [ ] **evil** 形①邪悪な ②有害な，不吉な 名①邪悪 ②害，わざわい，不幸 副悪く

- [ ] **examine** 動試験する，調査［検査］する，診察する

- [ ] **excellent** 形優れた，優秀な

- [ ] **except** 前〜を除いて，〜のほかは **except for** 〜を除いて，〜がなければ 接〜ということを除いて

- [ ] **excessive** 形度を超えた，行き過ぎた，極端な

- [ ] **excited** 動excite（興奮する）の過去，過去分詞 形興奮した，わくわくした **get excited** 興奮する

- [ ] **excitement** 名興奮（すること）

- [ ] **excuse oneself** 辞退する，中座する

- [ ] **expect** 動予期［予測］する，（当然のこととして）期待する

- [ ] **explain** 動説明する，明らかにする，釈明［弁明］する

- [ ] **explanation** 名①説明，解説，釈明 ②解釈，意味

- [ ] **eye** 熟**lay eyes on** 〜に目を留める **right before one's eyes** 目の前で

F

- [ ] **face** 名①顔，顔つき ②外観，外見 ③（時計の）文字盤，（建物の）正面 動直面する，立ち向かう

- [ ] **fact** 熟**as a matter of fact** 実際は，実のところ **in fact** つまり，実は，要するに

- [ ] **fail** 動①失敗する，落第する［させる］ ②《– to 〜》〜し損なう，〜できない ③失望させる 名失敗，落第点

- [ ] **fair** 形①正しい，公平［正当］な ②快晴の ③色白の，金髪の ④かなりの ⑤《古》美しい 副①公平に，きれいに ②見事に

- [ ] **faithful** 形忠実な，正確な

- [ ] **fall** 熟**fall against** 〜に倒れ込む **fall dead** 倒れて死ぬ **fall forward** 前のめりになる **fall off** （離れて）落ちる，低下する **fall on** 〜に降りかかる，〜に行き当たる **fall to the ground** 転ぶ，地面に落ちる **fall to work** 仕事を始める

- [ ] **fallen** 動fall（落ちる）の過去分詞 形落ちた，倒れた

- [ ] **family ties** 家族の絆

- [ ] **far** 熟**as far as** 〜と同じくらい遠く，〜まで，〜する限り（では） **by far** はるかに，断然 **far away** 遠く離れて **far from** 〜から遠い，〜どころか **how far** どこまで **so far** 今までのところ

- [ ] **fast asleep** ぐっすり眠っている

WORD LIST

□ **father** 名 ①父親 ②先祖, 創始者

□ **favor** 名 ①好意, えこひいき ②格別のはからい 動好意を示す, 賛成する

□ **fear** 名 ①恐れ ②心配, 不安 **in fear** おどおどして, ビクビクして 動 ①恐れる ②心配する

□ **fed** 動 feed (食物を与える) の過去, 過去分詞

□ **feed** 動 ①食物を与える ②供給する 名 ①飼育, 食事 ②供給

□ **feel** 動感じる, (〜と) 思う **feel better** 気分がよくなる **feel low** 気分が落ち込んでいる **feel sorry for** 〜をかわいそうに思う, 〜を申し訳なく思う

□ **feeling** 動 feel (感じる) の現在分詞 名 ①感じ, 気持ち ②触感, 知覚 ③同情, 思いやり, 感受性 **hard feelings** 悪感情 形感じる, 感じやすい, 情け深い

□ **feet** 熟 **get to one's feet** 立ち上がる

□ **fellow** 名 ①仲間, 同僚 ②人, やつ 形仲間の, 同士の

□ **fever** 名 ①熱気, 熱狂 ②熱病 動発熱させる, 熱狂させる

□ **fight** 動 (〜と) 戦う, 争う 名 ①戦い, 争い, けんか ②闘志, ファイト

□ **figure** 名 ①人 [物] の姿, 形 ②図 (形) ③数字 動 ①描写する, 想像する ②計算する ③目立つ, (〜として) 現れる **figure out** 理解する, 〜であるとわかる, (原因などを) 解明する

□ **final** 形最後の, 決定的な 名 ①最後のもの ②期末 [最終] 試験 ③《-s》決勝戦

□ **find** 動 ①見つける ②(〜と) わかる, 気づく, 〜と考える ③得る **find out** 見つけ出す, 気がつく, 知る, 調べる, 解明する

□ **finding** 動 find (見つける) の現在分詞 名 ①発見 ②《-s》発見物, 調査結果 ③《-s》認定, 決定, 答申

□ **fine** 形 ①元気な ②美しい, りっぱな, 申し分ない, 結構な

□ **finished** 動 finish (終わる) の過去, 過去分詞 形 ①終わった, 仕上がった ②洗練された ③もうだめになった

□ **fire** 熟 **catch fire** 火がつく, 引火する

□ **fireplace** 名暖炉

□ **firm** 名会社, 事務所 形堅い, しっかりした, 断固とした 副しっかりと

□ **firmly** 副しっかりと, 断固として

□ **first** 熟 **at first** 最初は, 初めのうちは **for the first time** 初めて

□ **fit** 形 ①適当な, 相応な ②体の調子がよい 動合致 [適合] する, 合致させる 名発作, けいれん, 一時的興奮

□ **fix** 動 ①固定する [させる] ②修理する ③決定する ④用意する, 整える

□ **flat** 形 ①平らな ②しぼんだ, 空気の抜けた 副 ①平らに, 平たく ②きっかり 名 ①平面, 平地 ②アパート

□ **fly away** 飛び去る

□ **follow** 動 ①ついていく, あとをたどる ②(〜の) 結果として起こる ③(忠告などに) 従う ④理解できる

□ **following** 動 follow (ついていく) の現在分詞 形《the -》次の, 次に続く 名《the -》下記のもの, 以下に述べるもの

□ **fool** 名 ①ばか者, おろかな人 ②道化師 動ばかにする, だます, ふざける

□ **foolish** 形おろかな, ばかばかしい

□ **foot** 名 ①足, 足取り ②(山などの) ふもと, (物の) 最下部, すそ ③フィート《長さの単位。約30cm》 **set foot** 足を踏み入れる

□ **force** 名力, 勢い 動 ①強制する, 力ずくで〜する, 余儀なく〜させる ②押しやる, 押し込む

□ **form** 名 ①形, 形式 ②書式 動形づくる

□ **former** 形 ①前の, 先の, 以前の ②

THE BEST SHORT STORIES OF EDGAR ALLAN POE

《the –》(二者のうち) 前者の

☐ **formerly** 副 元は, 以前は

☐ **fort** 名 砦, 要塞

☐ **Fort Moultrie** モールトリー要塞《アメリカのサリヴァン島にある要塞》

☐ **forth** 副 前へ, 外へ

☐ **forward** 形 ①前方の, 前方へ向かう ②将来の ③先の 副 ①前方に ②将来に向けて ③先へ, 進んで 動 ①転送する ②進める 名 前衛

☐ **frame** 名 骨組み, 構造, 額縁 動 形づくる, 組み立てる

☐ **French** 形 フランス(人・語)の 名 ①フランス語 ②《the –》フランス人

☐ **Frenchman** 名 フランス人の男, フランス人

☐ **frequently** 副 頻繁に, しばしば

☐ **friendly** 形 親しみのある, 親切な, 友情のこもった 副 友好的に, 親切に

☐ **friendship** 名 友人であること, 友情

☐ **front** 熟 in front of ～の前に, ～の正面に

☐ **frozen** 動 freeze (凍る) の過去分詞 形 ①凍った ②冷淡な

☐ **full** 形 ①満ちた, いっぱいの, 満期の ②完全な, 盛りの, 充実した be full of hot air ナンセンスなことばかり言う 名 全部

☐ **fun** 熟 have fun with ～ ～と楽しむ, ～でふざける make fun of ～を物笑いの種にする, からかう

☐ **further** 形 いっそう遠い, その上の, なおいっそうの 副 いっそう遠く, その上に, もっと 動 促進する

☐ **fury** 名 激しさ, 激怒, 激情

G

☐ **gallows** 名 絞首台

☐ **gather** 動 ①集まる, 集める ②生じる, 増す ③推測する

☐ **general** 形 ①全体の, 一般の, 普通の ②おおよその ③(職位の) 高い, 上級の in general 一般に, たいてい 名 大将, 将軍

☐ **German** 形 ドイツ(人・語)の 名 ①ドイツ人 ②ドイツ語

☐ **get** 動 ①得る, 手に入れる ②(ある状態に) なる, いたる ③わかる, 理解する ④～させる, ～を(…の状態に)する ⑤(ある場所に) 達する, 着く get along [人と] 仲が良い, うまくやっていく get away 逃げる, 離れる get back 戻る, 帰る get ～ back ～を取り返す[戻す] get better (病気などが) 良くなる get close 近づく get down 降りる, 着地する, 身をかがめる get excited 興奮する get hold of ～を手に入れる, ～をつかむ get home 家に着く[帰る] get in 中に入る, 乗り込む get into ～に入る, ～に巻き込まれる get out 取り出す, 抜き出す get started 始める get there そこに到着する, 目的を達成する get to one's feet 立ち上がる get up 起き上がる, 立ち上がる

☐ **give** 熟 give oneself up to ～に身を委ねる give up あきらめる, やめる, 引き渡す give way to ～に変わる, 抑え切れずに～する

☐ **go** 熟 go about 歩き回る go by (時が) 過ぎる, ～のそばを通る go down 下に降りる go home 帰宅する go in 中に入る, 開始する go into ～に入る, (仕事) に就く go on 続く, 続ける, 進み続ける go on to ～に移る, ～に取り掛かる go out 外出する, (火・明かりが) 消える go over ～を越える, ～を調べる, ～をきれいにする go over to ～の前に[へ] 行く, ～に出向いて行く go through 通り抜ける, 一つずつ順番に検討する go to bed 床につく, 寝る go up ①～に上がる, 登る ②～に近づく, 出かける go up in smoke 煙と消える go up to ～まで行く, 近づく go with ～と一緒に行く, ～と調和する, ～にとて

126

WORD LIST

も似合う **let go of** 〜から手を離す，〜を記憶から取り除く **ready to go** すっかり準備が整った

- **goat** 图 ヤギ(山羊)
- **god** 熟 **My God.** おや，まあ **in the name of God**《疑問詞を強めて》一体(全体)
- **gold** 图 金，金貨，金製品，金色 形 金の，金製の，金色の
- **gold money** 金貨
- **goodness** 图 ①善良さ，よいところ ②優秀 ③神《婉曲表現》
- **gotten** 動 get(得る)の過去分詞
- **grand** 形 雄大な，壮麗な
- **grave** 图 墓 形 重要な，厳粛な，落ち着いた
- **greatly** 副 大いに
- **grow into** 次第に〜になる
- **growth** 图 成長，発展 形 成長している
- **guilt** 图 罪，有罪，犯罪

H

- **hah** 間《驚き・疑い・喜びなどを表す》おや，まあ
- **hand** 图 ①手 ②(時計の)針 ③援助の手，助け **on the other hand** 一方，他方では **raise one's hand against** 〜に手を上げる 動 手渡す
- **hang head down** 頭を下にしてぶら下がる
- **hanging** 動 hang(かかる)の現在分詞 形 かかった，ぶら下がった 图 ①絞首刑 ②壁かけ
- **hangman** 图 絞首刑執行人
- **happiness** 图 幸せ，喜び
- **hard feelings** 悪感情
- **hard to** 〜し難い
- **harden** 動 固める，固くする，頑固にする

- **hardly** 副 ①ほとんど〜でない，わずかに ②厳しく，かろうじて
- **harm** 图 害，損害，危害 動 傷つける，損なう
- **harsh** 形 厳しい，とげとげしい，不快な
- **hate** 動 嫌う，憎む，(〜するのを)いやがる 图 憎しみ
- **hatred** 图 憎しみ，毛嫌い
- **have** 熟 **have a hard time 〜ing** 〜するのに苦労する **have fun with** 〜 〜と楽しむ，〜でふざける **have no choice but to** 〜するしかない **have no time to do** 〜する時間がない **have no way of doing** 〜するすべがない，〜しようがない **have nothing to do with** 〜と何の関係もない
- **he** 代 彼は[が]
- **head** 图 ①頭 ②先頭 ③長，指導者 動 向かう，向ける **hang head down** 頭を下にしてぶら下がる
- **heart** 图 ①心臓，胸 ②心，感情，ハート ③中心，本質 **lie at the heart of** 〜の中心にある
- **heart-warming** 形 心温まる，ほほえましい
- **heat** 图 ①熱，暑さ ②熱気，熱意，激情 動 熱する，暖める
- **heaven** 图 ①天国 ②天国のようなところ[状態]，楽園 ③空 ④《H-》神 **in heaven's name**(疑問詞を強めて)一体全体
- **heavy** 形 重い，激しい，つらい
- **height** 图 ①高さ，身長 ②《the −》絶頂，真っ盛り ③高台，丘
- **hell** 图 地獄，地獄のようなところ[状態]
- **help** 動 ①助ける，手伝う ②給仕する **cannot help 〜ing** 〜せずにはいられない **help in** 〜に役立つ **help 〜 to …** 〜が…するのを助ける 图 助け，手伝い
- **Henri Duval** 图 アンリ・デュヴァ

127

THE BEST SHORT STORIES OF EDGAR ALLAN POE

ル《人名》

- □ **here** 熟 **here and now** 今この場で **here and there** あちこちで **here are ~** こちらは~です。

- □ **hickory** 名 ヒッコリー《北米産クルミ科の木》

- □ **hid** 動 hide（隠れる）の過去, 過去分詞

- □ **hidden** 動 hide（隠れる）の過去分詞 形 隠れた, 秘密の

- □ **hide** 動 隠れる, 隠す, 隠れて見えない, 秘密にする

- □ **high** 形 ①高い ②気高い, 高価な 副 ①高く ②ぜいたくに 名 高い所

- □ **himself** 代 彼自身

- □ **hit** 動 ①打つ, なぐる ②（天災などが）襲う, 打撃を与える ③hitの過去, 過去分詞

- □ **hold** 動 ①つかむ, 持つ, 抱く ②保つ, 持ちこたえる ③収納できる, 入れることができる ④（会などを）開く **hold out** ①差し出す,（腕を）伸ばす ②持ちこたえる, 粘る, 耐える 名 ①つかむこと, 保有 ②支配［理解］力 **get［take］hold of ~**を手に入れる, ~をつかむ

- □ **home** 熟 **get home** 家に着く［帰る］ **go home** 帰宅する **make oneself at home** くつろぐ **on the way home** 帰宅途中に **take someone home**（人）を家まで送る

- □ **honor** 名 ①名誉, 光栄, 信用 ②節操, 自尊心 動 尊敬する, 栄誉を与える

- □ **hostel** 名 宿屋,（ユース）ホステル

- □ **Hot dog!** すごい！, やったー！

- □ **how** 熟 **How about ~?** ~はどうですか。~しませんか。 **how far** どこまで **how to** ~する方法 **no matter how** どんなに~であろうとも

- □ **however** 副 たとえ~でも 接 けれども, だが

- □ **huge** 形 巨大な, ばく大な

- □ **Huguenot** 名 ユグノー《16, 17世紀フランスの新教徒》

- □ **hum** 動 ブーンと音を立てる［うなる］, 鼻歌を歌う, 活気がある 間 うむ, ふうむ

- □ **human being** 人間, 人

- □ **hung** 動 hang（かかる）の過去, 過去分詞

- □ **hunting** 動 hunt（狩る）の現在分詞 名 狩り, 狩猟, ハンティング, 捜索 形 狩猟の

- □ **hut** 名 簡易住居, あばら屋, 山小屋

I

- □ **idea** 名 考え, 意見, アイデア, 計画

- □ **illness** 名 病気

- □ **image** 名 ①印象, 姿 ②画像, 映像 動 心に描く, 想像する

- □ **imagine** 動 想像する, 心に思い描く

- □ **imitate** 動 まねる, 模造する

- □ **importance** 名 重要性, 大切さ

- □ **impossible** 形 不可能な, できない, あり［起こり］えない

- □ **in** 前 ①《場所・位置・所属》~に［で・の］ ②《時》~の（時）に［の・で］, ~後（に）, ~の間（に） ③《方法・手段》~で ④~を身につけて, ~を着て ⑤~に関して, ~について ⑥《状態》~の状態で 副 中へ［に］, 内へ［に］

- □ **inch** 名 ①インチ《長さの単位。1/12フィート, 2.54cm》 ②少量

- □ **including** 動 include（含む）の現在分詞 前 ~を含めて, 込みで

- □ **increase** 動 増加［増強］する, 増やす, 増える 名 増加（量）, 増大

- □ **indeed** 副 ①実際, 本当に ②《強意》まったく 間 本当に, まさか

- □ **indicate** 動 ①指す, 示す,（道などを）教える ②それとなく言う ③きざしがある

Word List

- **influence** 名影響, 勢力 動影響をおよぼす
- **ink** 名インク 動(ペンなどに)インクをつける
- **innocent** 名無邪気な人, 罪のない人 形無邪気な, 無実の
- **insane** 形正気でない, 狂気の
- **insist** 動①主張する, 断言する ②要求する
- **insistence** 名主張, 無理強い
- **instantly** 副すぐに, 即座に
- **institution** 名①設立, 制定 ②制度, 慣習 ③協会, 公共団体
- **intelligent** 形頭のよい, 聡明な
- **intend** 動《－to－》～しようと思う, ～するつもりである
- **interested** 動interest(興味を起こさせる)の過去, 過去分詞 形興味を持った, 関心のある be interested in～に興味[関心]がある
- **interpreter** 名解説者, 通訳
- **interrupt** 動さえぎる, 妨害する, 口をはさむ
- **interview** 名会見, 面接 動会見[面接]する
- **iron** 名①鉄, 鉄製のもの ②アイロン 形鉄の, 鉄製の 動アイロンをかける
- **Isidore Musèt** イシドール・ミュゼ《人名》
- **issue** 名①問題, 論点 ②発行物 ③出口, 流出 動①(～から)出る, 生じる ②発行する
- **Italian** 形イタリア(人・語)の 名①イタリア人 ②イタリア語
- **itself** 代それ自体, それ自身

J

- **jewel** 名宝石, 貴重な人[物] 動宝石で飾る

- **joke** 名冗談, ジョーク 動冗談を言う, ふざける, からかう
- **judge** 動判決を下す, 裁く, 判断する, 評価する 名裁判官, 判事, 審査員
- **Jules Mignand** 名ジュール・ミニョー《人名》
- **jump into** ～に飛び込む
- **jump on** ～に飛びかかる
- **Jupiter** 名ジュピター《人名》

K

- **keep** 動①とっておく, 保つ, 続ける ②(～を…に)しておく ③飼う, 養う ④経営する ⑤守る keep ... from ～ing ...に～させない keep to oneself 人付き合いを避ける
- **keeping** 動keep(とっておく)の現在分詞 名①保管, 保存 ②調和, 一致
- **kid** 名子ヤギ
- **killer** 名殺人者[犯]
- **killing** 動kill(の殺す)の現在分詞 名殺害, 殺人 形①人を殺す, 植物を枯らす ②死ぬほどくたびれる
- **kind** 形親切な, 優しい 名種類
- **kindly** 形①親切な, 情け深い, 思いやりのある ②(気候などの)温和な, 快い 副親切に, 優しく
- **knife** 名ナイフ, 小刀, 包丁, 短剣
- **knock** 動ノックする, たたく, ぶつける 名打つこと, 戸をたたくこと[音]
- **know** 熟as you know ご存知のとおり know of ～について知っている you know ご存知のとおり, そうでしょう
- **knowing** 動know(知っている)の現在分詞 形物知りの, 故意の

THE BEST SHORT STORIES OF EDGAR ALLAN POE

L

- □ **laid** 動 lay (置く) の過去, 過去分詞
- □ **lantern** 名 手提げランプ, ランタン
- □ **lap** 名 ひざ
- □ **large** 熟 at large 全体として, 広く
- □ **last** 形 ①《the –》最後の ②この前の, 先〜 ③最新の 副 ①最後に ②この前 名《the –》最後 (のもの), 終わり at last ついに, とうとう 動 続く, 持ちこたえる
- □ **lasting** 動 last (続く) の現在分詞 形 長持ちする, 永続する
- □ **lay** 動 ①置く, 横たえる, 敷く ②整える ③卵を産む ④lie (横たわる) の過去 lay eyes on 〜に目を留める, 〜を見る [見つける] lay out きちんと並べる, 陳列する
- □ **lead** 動 ①導く, 案内する ②(生活を) 送る lead the way 先に立って導く, 案内する, 率先する lead to 〜に至る, 〜に通じる, 〜を引き起こす 名 ①鉛 ②先導, 指導
- □ **learn** 動 学ぶ, 習う, 教わる, 知識 [経験] を得る
- □ **least** 形 いちばん小さい, 最も少ない 副 いちばん小さく, 最も少なく 名 最小, 最少 at least 少なくとも
- □ **leave** 熟 leave for 〜に向かって出発する leave in 〜をそのままにしておく leave 〜 alone 〜をそっとしておく
- □ **led** 動 lead (導く) の過去, 過去分詞
- □ **left-handed** 形 左ききの, 左きき用の
- □ **length** 名 長さ, 縦, たけ, 距離
- □ **lent** 動 lend (貸す) の過去, 過去分詞
- □ **L'Espanaye** 名 レスパネ《人名》
- □ **less** 形 〜より小さい [少ない] 副 〜より少なく, 〜ほどでなく less and less だんだん少なく〜, ますます〜でなく more or less 多少, 多かれ少なかれ

- □ **lesson** 名 ①授業, 学科, 課, けいこ ②教訓, 戒め teach someone a lesson (人) にお説教をする, (人) を懲らしめる
- □ **let** 熟 Let me see. ええと。 let go of 〜から手を離す, 〜を記憶から取り除く let in 〜を招き入れる, 〜を中に入れる let us 私たちに〜させてください, 〜しましょう
- □ **lie** 動 ①うそをつく ②横たわる, 寝る ③(ある状態に) ある, 存在する lie at the heart of 〜の中心にある 名 うそ, 詐欺
- □ **lieutenant** 名 ①中尉, 少尉 ②代理, 副官
- □ **Lieutenant G___** G___ 中尉
- □ **life** 名 ①生命, 生物 ②一生, 生涯, 人生 ③生活, 暮らし, 世の中 for the life of me どうしても
- □ **lift** 動 ①持ち上げる, 上がる ②取り除く, 撤廃する 名 ①持ち上げること ②エレベーター, リフト
- □ **light** 名 光, 明かり come to light 明らかになる 動 火をつける, 照らす, 明るくする
- □ **lightning** 名 電光, 雷, 稲妻
- □ **like** 熟 like this このような, こんなふうに look like 〜のように見える, 〜に似ている would like to 〜したいと思う
- □ **likely** 形 ①ありそうな, (〜) しそうな ②適当な 副 たぶん, おそらく
- □ **liking** 動 like (好む) の現在分詞 名 好み, 趣味
- □ **line** 名 ①線, 糸, 電話線 ②(字の) 行, ③列, (電車の) 〜線 動 ①線を引く ②整列する
- □ **lip** 名 唇, 《-s》口
- □ **lit** 動 light (火をつける) の過去, 過去分詞
- □ **little** 形 ①小さい, 幼い ②少しの, 短い ③ほとんど〜ない, 《a –》少しはある 名 少し (しか), 少量 little by little 少しずつ 副 全然〜ない, 《a –》

130

WORD LIST

少しはある

- □ **living** 動 live (住む) の現在分詞 名 生計, 生活 形 ①生きている, 現存の ②使用されている ③そっくりの

- □ **location** 名 位置, 場所

- □ **logical** 形 論理学の, 論理的な

- □ **long** 動 思いこがれる, 熱望する 副 長く, ~にわたって **all day long** 一日中, 終日 **for so long** 長年にわたって

- □ **longboat** 名 長艇, ロングボート

- □ **look** 熟 **look after** ~の世話をする, ~に気をつける **look around** 見回す **look around for** ~を捜し求める **look down** 見下ろす **look down at** ~に目[視線]を落とす **look for** ~を探す **look in** 中を見る, 立ち寄る **look into** ~を調べる, ~のぞき込む **look like** ~のように見える, ~に似ている **look through** ~をのぞき込む **look to** ~しようとする **look up** 見上げる, 調べる **take a look at** ~を調べる

- □ **loose** 形 自由な, ゆるんだ, あいまいな 動 ほどく, 解き放つ

- □ **lord** 名 首長, 主人, 領主, 貴族, 上院議員

- □ **Lord above** 何ということだ, びっくりした

- □ **lose** 熟 **lose no time** すぐに~する **lose sight of** ~を見失う

- □ **loss** 熟 ①損失(額・物), 損害, 浪費 ②失敗, 敗北 **at a loss** 途方に暮れて

- □ **love** 名 愛, 愛情, 思いやり 動 愛する, 恋する, 大好きである

- □ **lovely** 形 愛らしい, 美しい, すばらしい

- □ **loving** 動 love (愛する) の現在分詞 形 愛する, 愛情のこもった

- □ **low** 熟 **feel low** 気分が落ち込んでいる

- □ **lower** 形 もっと低い, 下級の, 劣った 動 下げる, 低くする

- □ **lying** 動 lie (うそをつく・横たわる)

の現在分詞 形 ①うそをつく, 虚偽の ②横になっている 名 ①うそをつくこと, 虚言, 虚偽 ②横たわること

M

- □ **mad** 形 ①気の狂った ②逆上した, 理性をなくした ③ばかげた ④(~に)熱狂[熱中]して, 夢中の

- □ **Madame** ~夫人《フランス(系)女性に用いる》

- □ **Madame L.** 名 レスパネ夫人《L.は L'Espanaye の略》

- □ **made** 熟 **be made of** ~でできて[作られて]いる **be made up of** ~で構成されている

- □ **Mademoiselle** 名 ~嬢《フランス(系)女性に用いる》

- □ **Mademoiselle L.** 名 レスパネ嬢《L.は L'Espanaye の略》

- □ **madman** 名 ①狂人 ②常軌を逸した人

- □ **madness** 名 狂気, 熱中

- □ **main** 形 主な, 主要な

- □ **mainland** 名 本土, 大陸

- □ **make** 熟 **make a mistake** 間違いをする **make fun of** ~を物笑いの種にする, からかう **make noise** 音を立てる **make oneself at home** くつろぐ **make out** 作り上げる, 理解する **make sail** 帆を張る **make sense** 意味をなす, よくわかる **make up** 作り出す, 考え出す, ~を構成[形成]する **make up one's mind** 決心する **what to make of** ~をどう判断するか

- □ **Maker** 名 創造主, 神

- □ **Malta** 名 マルタ《国名》

- □ **Maltese** 形 マルタ(島・人)の 名 マルタ人

- □ **man** 名 男性, 人, 人類

- □ **manage** 動 ①動かす, うまく処理する ②経営[管理]する, 支配する

THE BEST SHORT STORIES OF EDGAR ALLAN POE

③どうにか～する

☐ **manner** 名①方法，やり方 ②態度，様子 ③《-s》行儀，作法，生活様式

☐ **mark** 名①印，記号，跡 ②点数 ③特色 動①印［記号］をつける ②採点する ③目立たせる

☐ **marry** 動結婚する

☐ **master** 名主人，雇い主，師，名匠 動①修得する ②～の主となる

☐ **Master Will** ウィル旦那

☐ **matching** 形調和する

☐ **material** 形①物質の，肉体的な ②不可欠な，重要な 名材料，原料

☐ **matter** 熟a matter of ～の問題 as a matter of fact 実際は，実のところ no matter how どんなに～であろうとも

☐ **may** 助①～かもしれない ②～してもよい，～できる may well ～するのももっともだ，多分～だろう 名《M-》5月

☐ **mean** 動①意味する ②（～のつもりで）言う，意図する ③～するつもりである 形①卑怯な，けちな，意地悪な ②中間の 名中間，中位

☐ **meaning** 名①意味，趣旨 ②重要性

☐ **means** 熟by means of（手段として）～によって

☐ **measure** 動①測る，（～の）寸法がある ②評価する 名①寸法，測定，計量，単位 ②程度，基準 tape measure 巻き尺

☐ **melancholy** 形もの悲しい，憂うつな，ふさぎ込んだ 名哀愁，憂うつ，うつ病

☐ **memory** 名記憶（力），思い出

☐ **men** 名man（男性）の複数

☐ **mention** 動（～について）述べる，言及する 名言及，陳述

☐ **meter** 名メートル《長さの単位》

☐ **method** 名①方法，手段 ②秩序，体系

☐ **middle** 名中間，最中 in the middle of ～の真ん中［中ほど］に 形中間の，中央の

☐ **might** 助《mayの過去》①～かもしれない ②～してもよい，～できる 名力，権力

☐ **mighty** 副ひどく，とてつもなく

☐ **mile** 名①マイル《長さの単位。1,609m》②《-s》かなりの距離

☐ **mind** 名①心，精神，考え ②知性 make up one's mind 決心する 動①気にする，いやがる ②気をつける，用心する mind one's own business いらぬおせっかいをしない Never mind. 気にするな。

☐ **minute** 名①（時間の）分 ②ちょっとの間 形ごく小さい，細心の

☐ **misanthropy** 名人間嫌い

☐ **missing** 動miss（失敗する）の現在分詞 形欠けている，行方不明の

☐ **misspelling** 名つづり間違い，スペルミス

☐ **mistaken** 動mistake（間違える）の過去分詞 形誤った

☐ **moment** 名①瞬間，ちょっとの間 ②（特定の）時，時期 at the moment 今は for a moment 少しの間 for the moment 差し当たり，当座は

☐ **monk** 名修道士，僧

☐ **monkey** 名サル（猿）動ふざける，いたずらをする

☐ **more** 熟more or less 多少，多かれ少なかれ more than ～以上 more than anything 何よりも no more もう～ない not ～ any more もう［これ以上］～ない once more もう一度

☐ **motive** 名動機，目的，モチーフ

☐ **mouth** 名①口 ②言葉，発言 down in the mouth 落ち込んで

☐ **movement** 名①動き，運動 ②《-s》行動 ③引っ越し ④変動

☐ **much** 形（量・程度が）多くの，多量の 副①とても，たいへん ②《比較級

132

WORD LIST

・最上級を修飾して》ずっと，はるかに **in much the same way** ほぼ同じように **too much** 過度に 名多量，たくさん，重要なもの

□ **murder** 名人殺し，殺害，殺人事件 動殺す

□ **murderer** 名殺人犯

□ **myrtle** 名ギンバイカ，ヒメツルニチソウ《植物》

□ **mystery** 名①神秘，不可思議 ②推理小説，ミステリー

N

□ **nail** 名①爪 ②くぎ，びょう 動くぎを打つ，くぎづけにする

□ **narrow** 形①狭い ②限られた 動狭くなる［する］

□ **nature** 熟 **by nature** 生まれつき **in nature**《疑問の強意》一体

□ **nearby** 形近くの，間近の 副近くで，間近で

□ **nearly** 副①近くに，親しく ②ほとんど，あやうく

□ **necessarily** 副①必ず，必然的に，やむを得ず ②《not-》必ずしも～でない

□ **necessary** 形必要な，必然の 名《-s》必要品，必需品

□ **neck** 名首，（衣服の）えり

□ **neighboring** 形隣の，近所の

□ **neither** 形どちらの～も…でない 代《2者のうち》どちらも～でない 副《否定文に続いて》～も…しない

□ **nerve** 名①神経 ②気力，精力 ③《-s》神経過敏，臆病，憂うつ

□ **New Orleans** 名ニューオーリンズ《アメリカ，ルイジアナ州の都市》

□ **Newfoundland** 名①ニューファンドランド《カナダの島・州》②ニューファンドランド犬

□ **newspaper** 名新聞（紙）

□ **noise** 名騒音，騒ぎ，物音 **make noise** 音を立てる

□ **noisy** 形①騒々しい，やかましい ②けばけばしい

□ **none** 代（～の）何も［誰も・少しも］…ない

□ **normal** 形普通の，平均の，標準的な 名平常，標準，典型

□ **northeast** 名北東，北東部 形北東の，北東部の 副北東に［へ］

□ **note** 名①メモ，覚え書き ②注釈 ③注意，注目 ④手形 動①書き留める ②注意［注目］する

□ **nothing** 代何も～ない［しない］ **for nothing** ただで，無料で，むだに **have nothing to do with** ～と何の関係もない **nothing but** ただ～だけ，～にすぎない，～のほかは何も…ない

□ **notice** 名①注意 ②通知 ③公告 **take notice of** ～に気付く 動①気づく，認める ②通告する

□ **now** 熟 **here and now** 今この場で **now and then** ときどき **now that** 今や～だから，～からには **right now** 今すぐに，たった今

□ **nut** 名木の実，ナッツ

O

□ **object** 名①物，事物 ②目的物，対象 動反対する，異議を唱える

□ **obviously** 副明らかに，はっきりと

□ **occasion** 名①場合，（特定の）時 ②機会，好機 ③理由，根拠

□ **occupy** 動①占領する，保有する ②居住する ③占める ④（職に）つく，従事する

□ **occur** 動（事が）起こる，生じる，（考えなどが）浮かぶ

□ **odd** 形①奇妙な ②奇数の ③（一対のうちの）片方の

□ **Odenheimer** 名オルデンハイメ

133

THE BEST SHORT STORIES OF EDGAR ALLAN POE

ル《人名》

□ **off** 熟 come off 取れる, はずれる
fall off (離れて) 落ちる, 低下する
take off (衣服を) 脱ぐ

□ **offer** 動 申し出る, 申し込む, 提供す
る 名 提案, 提供

□ **officer** 名 役人, 公務員, 警察官

□ **once** 熟 all at once 突然, 出し抜
けに at once すぐに, 同時に once
and for all これを最後にきっぱりと
once in a while たまに, 時々 once
more もう一度

□ **only** 形 唯一の 副 ①単に, ～にす
ぎない, ただ～だけ ②やっと 接 た
だし, だがしかし

□ **ooooh** 間《驚き・喜びなどを表す》
おおっ, わあっ

□ **opal** 名 オパール

□ **opening** 動 open (開く) の現在分
詞 名 開いた所, 穴

□ **opinion** 名 意見, 見識, 世論, 評判

□ **opposite** 形 反対の, 向こう側の
副 ～の向こう側に 名 反対の人[物]

□ **orangutan** 名 オランウータン

□ **organization** 名 ①組織 (化), 編
成, 団体, 機関 ②有機体, 生物

□ **original** 形 ①始めの, 元の, 本来の
②独創的な 名 原型, 原文

□ **other** 熟 on the other hand 一方,
他方では the other day 先日

□ **outburst** 名 爆発, 噴出

□ **outer** 形 外の, 外側の

□ **outing** 動 out (追い出す) の現在分
詞 名 外出, 遠出, 遠足

□ **outline** 名 ①外形, 輪郭 ②概略

□ **oval** 形 卵形の, 楕円形の 名 ①卵型,
楕円形 ②(楕円形の) 競技場

□ **over** 熟 all over again もう一度,
繰り返して be over 終わる go over
～を越える, ～を調べる, ～をきれい
にする go over to ～の前に[へ]行く,
～に出向いて行く reach over 手を
伸ばす turn over ひっくり返る [返

す], (ページを) めくる, 思いめぐら
す, 引き渡す watch over 見守る, 見
張る

□ **overall** 形 総体的な, 全面的な 副
全般的に見れば 名 オーバーオール,
作業着

□ **overcame** 動 overcome (勝つ) の
過去

□ **owe** 動 ①(～を) 負う, (～を人の)
お陰とする ②(金を) 借りている, (人
に対して～の) 義務がある

□ **own** 熟 on one's own 自力で

□ **owner** 名 持ち主, オーナー

P

□ **package** 名 包み, 小包, パッケー
ジ 動 包装する, 荷造りする

□ **parchment** 名 羊皮紙, 羊皮紙文
書

□ **Paris** 名 パリ《フランスの首都》

□ **part** 名 ①部分, 割合 ②役目 for
one's part ～に関する限り play a
part 役目を果たす 動 分ける, 分か
れる, 別れる part with ～を手放す,
～と別れる

□ **particularly** 副 特に, とりわけ

□ **partly** 副 一部分は, ある程度は

□ **party** 名 ①パーティー, 会, 集まり
②派, 一行, 隊, 一味 ③(ある行動の)
関係者 third party 第三者

□ **pass** 動 ①過ぎる, 通る ②(年月
が) たつ ③(試験に) 合格する ④手
渡す pass by ～のそばを通る [通り
過ぎる] pass out 気絶する pass
through ～を通る, 通行する 名 ①
通過 ②入場券, 通行許可 ③合格, パ
ス

□ **past** 形 過去の, この前の 名 過去 (の
出来事) 前《時間・場所》～を過ぎて,
～を越して 副 通り越して, 過ぎて

□ **patient** 形 我慢 [忍耐] 強い, 根気
のある 名 病人, 患者

134

WORD LIST

- **patiently** 副 我慢強く, 根気よく
- **Paul Dumas** 名 ポール・デュマ《人名》
- **Pauline Dubourg** 名 ポーリン・デュブール《人名》
- **pay** 動 ①支払う, 払う, 報いる, 償う ②割に合う, ペイする **pay attention to** ~に注意を払う 名 給料, 報い
- **peak** 名 頂点, 最高点 動 最高になる, ピークに達する
- **perfectly** 副 完全に, 申し分なく
- **perhaps** 副 たぶん, ことによると
- **personality** 名 人格, 個性
- **perversity** 名 つむじ曲り, 強情
- **pet** 名 ペット, お気に入り 形 お気に入りの, 愛がんの 動 かわいがる
- **physical** 形 ①物質の, 物理学の, 自然科学の ②身体の, 肉体の
- **pick** 熟 **come to pick up** ~を取りに来る **pick out** 拾い出す, えり抜く, 選び出す **pick up** 拾い上げる, 車で迎えに行く
- **picture** 名 ①絵, 写真,《-s》映画 ②イメージ, 事態, 状況, 全体像 動 描く, 想像する
- **piece** 名 ①一片, 部分 ②1個, 1本 ③作品
- **Pierre Moreau** 名 ピエール・モロー《人名》
- **pirate** 名 海賊 動 海賊行為を働く
- **pistol** 名 拳銃
- **place** 熟 **take place** 行われる, 起こる
- **plainly** 副 はっきりと, 明らかに
- **plaster** 名 しっくい, 壁土, 石膏 動 しっくいを塗る
- **pleasure** 名 喜び, 楽しみ, 満足, 娯楽
- **plunge** 動 ①飛び込む, 突入する ②(ある状態に)陥れる 名 突入, 突進
- **Pluto** 名 プルートー《ネコの名前》

- **pocket** 名 ①ポケット, 袋 ②所持金 動 ①ポケットに入れる ②着服する 形 携帯用の, 小型の
- **point** 熟 **at this point** 現在のところ **point of view** 考え方, 視点 **point out** 指し示す, 指摘する, 目を向ける, 目を向けさせる
- **poor** 形 ①貧しい, 粗末な, 貧弱な ②劣った, へたな ③不幸な, 哀れな, 気の毒な
- **poorly** 副 ①貧しく, 乏しく ②へたに
- **position** 名 ①位置, 場所, 姿勢 ②地位, 身分, 職 ③立場, 状況 動 置く, 配置する
- **possession** 名 ①所有(物) ②財産, 領土
- **possibility** 名 可能性, 見込み, 将来性
- **possible** 形 ①可能な ②ありうる, 起こりうる **as ~ as possible** できるだけ~
- **possibly** 副 ①あるいは, たぶん ②《否定文, 疑問文で》どうしても, できる限り, とても, なんとか
- **powerful** 形 力強い, 実力のある, 影響力のある
- **preparation** 名 ①準備, したく ②心構え
- **prepared** 形 準備[用意]のできた
- **present** 形 ①出席している, ある, いる ②現在の 名 ①《the -》現在 ②贈り物, プレゼント 動 ①紹介する ②現れる ③与える ④提出する, 述べる, 示す
- **preserve** 動 保存[保護]する, 保つ
- **press** 動 ①圧する, 押す, プレスする ②強要する, 迫る 名 ①圧迫, 押し, 切迫 ②出版物[社], 新聞
- **prevent** 動 ①妨げる, じゃまする ②予防する, 守る,《- ~ from …》~が…できない[しない]ようにする
- **previous** 形 前の, 先の

THE BEST SHORT STORIES OF EDGAR ALLAN POE

- [ ] **price** 名①値段, 代価 ②《-s》物価, 相場 動値段をつける, 値段を聞く
- [ ] **principal** 形主な, 第一の, 主要な, 重要な 名①長, 社長, 校長 ②主役, 主犯, 本人
- [ ] **prison** 名①刑務所, 監獄 ②監禁
- [ ] **probably** 副たぶん, あるいは
- [ ] **proceed** 動進む, 進展する, 続ける 名《-s》①結果 ②収益, 所得, 売却代金
- [ ] **process** 名①過程, 経過, 進行 ②手順, 方法, 製法, 加工
- [ ] **produce** 動①生産する, 製造する ②生じる, 引き起こす ③(物を)取り出す 名①生産額[物] ②結果
- [ ] **professor** 名教授, 師匠
- [ ] **projection** 名①突出, 突起 ②投影(図)
- [ ] **properly** 副適切に, きっちりと
- [ ] **proud** 形①自慢の, 誇った, 自尊心のある ②高慢な, 尊大な
- [ ] **pull** 熟pull on ～を引っ張る, 身につける, こぎ続ける pull out引き抜く, 引き出す, 取り出す
- [ ] **pulse** 名①脈拍 ②律動, 拍子 動脈打つ, 鼓動する
- [ ] **punctuate** 動①句読点をつける ②(演説など)を中断させる, (動作など)を交える
- [ ] **pure** 形①純粋な, 混じりけのない ②罪のない, 清い
- [ ] **push up** 押し上げる
- [ ] **put** 熟put away 片づける, 取っておく put back (もとの場所に)戻す, 返す put in ～の中に入れる put on ①～を身につける, 着る ②～を…の上に置く put ～ into … ～を…の状態にする, ～を…に突っ込む
- [ ] **puzzle** 名①難問, 当惑 ②パズル 動迷わせる, 当惑する[させる]

Q

- [ ] **quarter** 名①4分の1, 25セント, 15分, 3カ月 ②方面, 地域 ③部署 動4等分する
- [ ] **question** 名質問, 疑問, 問題 in question 問題の, 論争中の 動①質問する ②調査する ③疑う
- [ ] **questioning** 動question (質問する)の現在分詞 形疑うような 名質問, 尋問, 疑問
- [ ] **quickly** 副敏速に, 急いで
- [ ] **quietly** 副①静かに ②平穏に, 控えめに
- [ ] **quite** 熟not quite まったく～だというわけではない

R

- [ ] **rabbit** 名①ウサギ(兎), ウサギの毛皮 ②弱虫
- [ ] **raise** 動①上げる, 高める ②起こす ③～を育てる raise one's hand against ～に手を上げる
- [ ] **rather** 副①むしろ, かえって ②かなり, いくぶん, やや ③それどころか逆に rather than ～よりむしろ
- [ ] **ray** 名①光線, 放射線 ②光明
- [ ] **razor** 名(電気)かみそり
- [ ] **reach** 動①着く, 到着する, 届く ②手を伸ばして取る, (～を取ろうと)手を伸ばす reach down 手を下に伸ばす reach out [over] 手を伸ばす 名手を伸ばすこと, (手の)届く範囲
- [ ] **react** 動反応する, 対処する
- [ ] **reader** 名読者
- [ ] **reading** 動read (読む)の現在分詞 名読書, 読み物, 朗読
- [ ] **ready** 熟be ready to すぐに「いつでも」～できる, ～する構えで ready to go すっかり準備が整った
- [ ] **reality** 名現実, 実在, 真実(性)
- [ ] **realize** 動理解する, 実現する

WORD LIST

□ **reason** 名①理由 ②理性, 道理 ③正気, 分別 動①推論する ②説き伏せる

□ **reasoning** 名推理, 論法

□ **recover** 動①取り戻す, ばん回する ②回復する

□ **refer** 動①《–to ～》～に言及する, ～と呼ぶ, ～を指す ②～を参照する, ～に問い合わせる

□ **refuse** 動拒絶する, 断る 名くず, 廃物

□ **regard** 動①《～を…と》見なす ②尊敬する, 重きを置く ③関係がある 名注意, 関心 in regard to ～に関しては

□ **region** 名①地方, 地域 ②範囲

□ **regular** 形①規則的な, 秩序のある ②定期的な, 一定の, 習慣的

□ **relationship** 名関係, 関連, 血縁関係

□ **relief** 名(苦痛・心配などの)除去, 軽減, 安心, 気晴らし

□ **remove** 動①取り去る, 除去する ②(衣類を)脱ぐ

□ **rent** 動賃借りする rent out 賃貸する 名使用料, 賃貸料

□ **repeat** 動繰り返す 名繰り返し, 反復, 再演

□ **replace** 動①取り替える, 差し替える ②元に戻す

□ **reply** 動答える, 返事をする, 応答する 名答え, 返事, 応答

□ **represent** 動①表現する ②意味する ③代表する

□ **require** 動①必要とする, 要する ②命じる, 請求する

□ **respect** 名①尊敬, 尊重 ②注意, 考慮 in this respect この点において 動尊敬[尊重]する

□ **responsible** 形責任のある, 信頼できる, 確実な

□ **rest** 名①休息 ②安静 ③休止, 停止 ④《the –》残り 動①休む, 眠る ②休止する, 静止する ③(～に)基づいている ④(～の)ままである ⑤ある, 置かれている

□ **restless** 形落ち着かない, 不安な

□ **result** 名結果, 成り行き, 成績 動(結果として)起こる, 生じる, 結局～になる

□ **retain** 動①保つ, 持ち続ける ②覚えている

□ **return** 熟in return お返しとして return to ～に戻る, ～に帰る

□ **right** 熟all right 大丈夫で, よろしい, 申し分ない, わかった, 承知した right away すぐに right before one's eyes 目の前で right now 今すぐに, たった今

□ **ring** 名輪, 円形, 指輪

□ **rise** 動①昇る, 上がる ②生じる 名①上昇, 上がること ②発生

□ **rock** 名①岩, 岸壁, 岩石 ②揺れること, 動揺 動揺れる, 揺らす

□ **rod** 名棒, 竿

□ **rope** 名綱, なわ, ロープ 動なわで縛る

□ **rotten** 形①腐った, 堕落した ②不快な

□ **rub** 動①こする, こすって磨く ②すりむく 名摩擦

□ **ruby** 名ルビー 形ルビー色の, 真紅の

□ **rue** 名通り, ～街《フランス語》

□ **Rue Morgue** 名モルグ街

□ **run** 熟run around 走り回る run into (思いがけず)～に出会う, ～に駆け込む run on 走り続ける, 続くrun out of ～が不足する, ～を使い果たす run through 走り抜ける

□ **rush** 動突進する, せき立てる rush in ～に突入する, ～に駆けつける rush out of 急いで～から出てくる rush up 駆け上がる 名突進, 突撃, 殺到

□ **Russian** 名ロシア(人・語)の

137

THE BEST SHORT STORIES OF EDGAR ALLAN POE

图 ①ロシア人 ②ロシア語

S

- □ **sad-looking** 形 みじめな様子の
- □ **sadness** 图 悲しみ, 悲哀
- □ **safety** 图 安全, 無事, 確実
- □ **sail** 图 ①帆, 帆船 ②帆走, 航海 make sail 帆を張る 動 ①帆走する, 航海する, 出航する ②滑らかに飛ぶ
- □ **sailor** 图 船員, (ヨットの) 乗組員
- □ **sand** 图 ①砂 ②《-s》砂漠, 砂浜
- □ **sank** 動 sink (沈む) の過去
- □ **sapphire** 图 サファイア
- □ **satisfy** 動 ①満足させる, 納得させる ②(義務を) 果たす, 償う
- □ **say to oneself** ひとり言を言う, 心に思う
- □ **scarab** 图 ①コガネムシ ②スカラベ《古代エジプトで崇拝された神聖甲虫》
- □ **scream** 图 金切り声, 絶叫 動 叫ぶ, 金切り声を出す
- □ **scythe** 图 (長柄の草刈り用) 大鎌
- □ **seacoast** 图 海岸, 沿岸
- □ **search** 動 捜し求める, 調べる 图 捜査, 探索, 調査 in search of ~を探し求めて
- □ **second** 图 ①第2(の人[物]) ②(時間の) 秒, 瞬時 形 第2の, 2番の 副 第2に 動 後援する, 支持する
- □ **secret** 形 ①秘密の, 隠れた ②神秘の, 不思議な 图 秘密, 神秘
- □ **seem** 動 (~に) 見える, (~のように) 思われる seem to be ~であるように思われる
- □ **self** 图 ①自己, ~そのもの ②私利, 私欲, 利己主義 ③自我
- □ **send for** ~を呼びにやる, ~を呼び寄せる
- □ **send someone off** (人) を見送

る

- □ **sense** 图 ①感覚, 感じ ②《-s》意識, 正気, 本性 ③常識, 分別, センス ④意味 make sense 意味をなす, よくわかる 動 感じる, 気づく
- □ **sensible** 形 ①分別のある ②理にかなっている ③気づいている
- □ **sentence** 图 ①文 ②判決, 宣告 動 判決を下す, 宣告する
- □ **separate** 動 ①分ける, 分かれる, 隔てる ②別れる, 別れさせる 形 分かれた, 別れた, 別々の
- □ **series** 图 一続き, 連続, シリーズ
- □ **serious** 形 ①まじめな, 真剣な ②重大な, 深刻な, (病気などが) 重い
- □ **seriously** 副 ①真剣に, まじめに ②重大に
- □ **servant** 图 召使, 使用人, しもべ
- □ **set** 動 ①置く, 当てる, つける ②整える, 設定する ③(太陽・月などが) 沈む ④《~を…の状態に》する, させる ⑤setの過去, 過去分詞 set foot 足を踏み入れる 形 ①決められた, 固定した ②断固とした ③準備のできた 图 一そろい, セット
- □ **setting** 動 set (置く) の現在分詞 图 設定, 周囲の環境
- □ **settle** 動 ①安定する [させる], 落ち着く, 落ち着かせる ②《- in ~》~に移り住む, 定住する
- □ **sever** 動 切る, 切断する, 断つ
- □ **shake** 動 ①振る, 揺れる, 揺さぶる, 震える ②動揺させる shake off 振り払う 图 振ること
- □ **shape** 图 ①形, 姿, 型 ②状態, 調子 in the shape of ~の形をした 動 形づくる, 具体化する
- □ **sharp** 形 ①鋭い, とがった ②刺すような, きつい ③鋭敏な ④急な 副 ①鋭く, 急に ②(時間が) ちょうど
- □ **shave** 動 (ひげ・顔を) そる, 削る 图 ひげそり, 剃髪, 削り (くず)
- □ **shell** 图 ①貝がら, (木の実・卵など

WORD LIST

の) から ②(建物の) 骨組み

□ **shine** 動 ①光る, 輝く ②光らせる, 磨く 名光, 輝き

□ **shiny** 形 輝く, 光る

□ **shocking** 動 shock (ショックを与える) の現在分詞 形 衝撃的な, ショッキングな

□ **shone** 動 shine (光る) の過去, 過去分詞

□ **shook** 動 shake (振る) の過去

□ **short** 熟 in short 要約すると

□ **shortly** 副 まもなく, すぐに

□ **should** 助 ～すべきである, ～したほうがよい

□ **shoulder** 名肩 動肩にかつぐ, 肩で押し分けて進む

□ **shout** 動 叫ぶ, 大声で言う, どなりつける 名叫び, 大声, 悲鳴

□ **shut** 動 ①閉まる, 閉める, 閉じる ②たたむ ③閉じ込める ④shutの過去, 過去分詞

□ **shutter** 名 シャッター, 雨戸

□ **side** 名 側, 横, そば, 斜面 on each side それぞれの側に on either side of ～の両側に one side 片側 形 ①側面の, 横の ②副次的な side street わき道 動 (～の) 側につく, 賛成する

□ **sight** 熟 at the sight of ～を見るとすぐに lose sight of ～を見失う

□ **signature** 名書名, サイン

□ **silence** 名沈黙, 無言, 静寂 動沈黙させる, 静める

□ **silver** 名銀, 銀貨, 銀色 形銀製の

□ **similar** 形同じような, 類似した, 相似の

□ **similarity** 名類似(点), 相似

□ **simple** 形 ①単純な, 簡単な, 質素な ②単一の, 単独の ③普通の, ただの

□ **simply** 副 ①簡単に ②単に, ただ ③まったく, 完全に

□ **single** 形 ①たった1つの ②1人用の, それぞれの ③独身の ④片道の

□ **sit on** ～の上に乗る, ～の上に乗って動けないようにする

□ **skeleton** 名骨格, がい骨, 骨組み 形骨格の, 骨組みだけの, やせた

□ **skin** 名皮膚, 皮, 革(製品) 動皮をはぐ, すりむく

□ **skull** 名頭蓋骨, 頭, 頭脳

□ **sleep** 動 ①眠る, 寝る ②活動しない sleep off 眠って～を取り除く 名 ①睡眠, 冬眠 ②静止, 不活動

□ **slip** 動滑る, 滑らせる, 滑って転ぶ slip out そっと抜け出す 名滑ること

□ **slow-moving** 形動きの遅い[ゆるやかな]

□ **slowly** 副遅く, ゆっくり

□ **smile from ear to ear** 満面の笑みを浮かべる

□ **smoke** 動喫煙する, 煙を出す 名煙, 煙状のもの go up in smoke 煙と消える

□ **so** 熟 and so そこで, それだから, それで for so long 長年にわたって not so ～ as …… ～ほど～でない or so ～かそこらで so ～ as to …… するほど～で so far 今までのところ so ～ that … 非常に～なので… so that ～するために, それで, ～できるように so to speak いわば

□ **solve** 動解く, 解決する

□ **somebody** 代誰か, ある人

□ **someday** 副いつか, そのうち

□ **somehow** 副 ①どうにかこうにか, ともかく, 何とかして ②どういうわけか

□ **someone** 代ある人, 誰か take someone home (人) を家まで送る

□ **something** 代 ①ある物, 何か ②いくぶん, 多少 something to do 何か～する[すべき]こと

□ **sometimes** 副時々, 時たま

139

THE BEST SHORT STORIES OF EDGAR ALLAN POE

□ **somewhat** 副 いくらか, やや, 多少

□ **somewhere** 副 ①どこかへ[に] ②いつか, およそ

□ **soon** 熟 as soon as ～するとすぐ, ～するや否や

□ **soundly** 副 すこやかに, ぐっすりと

□ **source** 名 源, 原因, もと

□ **South Carolina** 名 サウスカロライナ《アメリカ南東部の州》

□ **southern** 形 南の, 南向きの, 南からの

□ **spade** 名 鋤, 踏みぐわ 動 鋤で掘り起こす, 耕す

□ **Spain** 名 スペイン《国名》

□ **Spaniard** 名 スペイン人

□ **Spanish** 形 スペイン (人・語) の 名 ①スペイン人 ②スペイン語

□ **speak** 熟 so to speak いわば speak of ～を口にする speak to ～と話す

□ **specimen** 名 見本, 実例

□ **speed** 名 速力, 速度

□ **spot** 名 ①地点, 場所, 立場 ②斑点, しみ on the spot その場で, ただちに 動 ①～を見つける ②点を打つ, しみをつける

□ **spread** 動 ①広がる, 広げる, 伸びる, 伸ばす ②塗る, まく, 散布する spread out 広げる, 展開する 名 広がり, 拡大

□ **spring** 名 ①春 ②泉, 源 ③ばね, ぜんまい 動 跳ねる, 跳ぶ

□ **St. Roch** 名 サン・ロック《地名》

□ **stair** 名 ①(階段の)1段 ②〈-s〉階段, はしご

□ **stand** 動 ①立つ, 立たせる, 立っている, ある ②耐える, 立ち向かう stand out 突き出る, 目立つ 名 ①台, 屋台, スタンド ②〈the -s〉観覧席 ③立つこと

□ **state** 名 あり様, 状態 動 述べる,

表明する

□ **step** 名 ①歩み, 1歩(の距離) ②段階 ③踏み段, 階段 動 歩む, 踏む

□ **stick** 名 棒, 杖 動 ①(突き)刺さる, 刺す ②くっつく, くっつける ③突き出る ④《受け身形で》いきづまる stick out of ～から突き出す

□ **stop by** 途中で立ち寄る, ちょっと訪ねる

□ **stop doing** ～するのをやめる

□ **storm** 名 ①嵐, 暴風雨 ②強襲 動 ①襲撃[強襲]する ②嵐が吹く ③突入する

□ **strangely** 副 奇妙に, 変に, 不思議なことに, 不慣れに

□ **stream** 名 ①小川, 流れ ②風潮 動 流れ出る, 流れる, なびく

□ **strength** 名 ①力, 体力 ②長所, 強み ③強度, 濃度

□ **strengthen** 動 強くする, しっかりさせる

□ **stretch** 動 引き伸ばす, 広がる, 広げる 名 伸ばす[伸びる]こと, 広がり

□ **strike** 動 ①打つ, ぶつかる ②(災害などが)急に襲う 名 打つこと, 打撃

□ **string** 名 ①ひも, 糸, 弦 ②一連, 一続き 動 糸[ひも]をつける, 弦を張る

□ **struck** 動 strike (打つ)の過去, 過去分詞

□ **struggle** 動 もがく, 奮闘する 名 もがき, 奮闘

□ **stuck** 動 stick (刺さる)の過去, 過去分詞

□ **stupid** 形 ばかな, おもしろくない

□ **subject** 名 ①話題, 議題, 主題 ②学科 ③題材, 対象 形 ①支配を受ける, 従属している ②(～を)受けやすい, (～む)必要とする be subject to ～の癖がある 動 服従させる

□ **succeed** 動 ①成功する ②(～の)跡を継ぐ

140

WORD LIST

□ **success** 名 成功, 幸運, 上首尾

□ **such** and such ～など such as たとえば～, ～のような such ～ that … 非常に～なので…

□ **suffer** 動 ①(苦痛・損害などを)受ける, こうむる ②(病気に)なる, 苦しむ, 悩む

□ **suggest** 動 ①提案する ②示唆する

□ **suit** 名 ①スーツ, 背広 ②訴訟 ③ひとそろい, 一組 動 ①適合する[させる] ②似合う

□ **Sullivan's Island** 名 サリヴァン島《アメリカ, チャールストン湾にある島》

□ **sun** 名《the –》太陽, 日

□ **suppose** 動 ①仮定する, 推測する ②《be -d to ～》～することになっている, ～するものである

□ **sure** 熟 for sure 確かに sure enough 思ったとおり, 確かに

□ **surprised** 動 surprise (驚かす)の過去, 過去分詞 形 驚いた

□ **surprisingly** 副 驚くほど(に), 意外にも

□ **swung** 動 swing (回転する)の過去, 過去分詞

T

□ **table** 名 ①テーブル, 食卓, 台 ②一覧表 動 卓上に置く, 棚上げにする

□ **tableland** 名 台地, 高原

□ **tailor** 名 仕立屋, テーラー 動 (服を)仕立てる, 注文で作る

□ **take** 熟 take a look at ～を調べる take care of ～の世話をする, ～面倒を見る, ～を管理する take control of ～を制御[管理]する, 支配する take hold of ～をつかむ, 捕らえる, 制する take notice of ～に気付く take off (衣服を)脱ぐ take out 取り出す, 持って帰る take out of ～

から出す, ～に連れ出す take place 行われる, 起こる take someone home (人)を家まで送る

□ **talk** 動 話す, 語る, 相談する 名 ①話, おしゃべり ②演説 ③《the –》話題

□ **tape** 名 テープ tape measure 巻き尺

□ **teach someone a lesson** (人)にお説教をする, (人)を懲らしめる

□ **tear** 熟 tear at ～を引き裂こうとする

□ **telescope** 名 望遠鏡

□ **tell** 熟 tell ～ to … ～に…するように言う to tell the truth 実は, 実を言えば

□ **tender** 形 柔らかい, もろい, 弱い, 優しい

□ **terribly** 副 ひどく

□ **terror** 名 ①恐怖 ②恐ろしい人[物]

□ **then** 副 その時(に・は), それから, 次に now and then ときどき 名 その時 形 その当時の

□ **there** 副 ①そこに[で・の], そこへ, あそこへ ②《– is [are] ～》～がある[いる] get there そこに到着する, 目的を達成する here and there あちこちで there is no doubt (～ということは)疑いない 名 そこ

□ **therefore** 副 したがって, それゆえ, その結果

□ **thick** 形 厚い, 密集した, 濃厚な 副 厚く, 濃く 名 最も厚い[強い・濃い]部分

□ **thin** 形 薄い, 細い, やせた, まばらな 副 薄く 動 薄く[細く]なる, 薄くする

□ **think** 熟 think better of it そうしない方が賢明だと思う think of ～のことを考える, ～を思いつく, 考え出す

□ **those who** ～する人々

□ **though** 接 ①～にもかかわらず, ～だが ②たとえ～でも as though

141

THE BEST SHORT STORIES OF EDGAR ALLAN POE

あたかも〜のように, まるで〜みたいに **副** しかし

□ **thoughtfulness** 名 思慮深さ, 心遣い

□ **throw** 動 投げる, 浴びせる, ひっかける **throw a person down** 人を転ばす **throw away** 〜を捨てる, 〜を無駄に費やす, 浪費する **throw down** 投げ出す, 放棄する **throw out** 放り出す 名 投げること, 投球

□ **thrown** 動 throw (投げる) の過去分詞

□ **thus** 副 ①このように ②これだけ ③かくて, だから

□ **tie** 動 結ぶ, 束縛する 名 ①結び (目) ②ネクタイ ③《-s》縁, きずな **family ties** 家族の絆

□ **time** 熟 **all the time** ずっと, いつも, その間ずっと **at that time** その時 **at the time** そのころ, 当時は **at times** 時には **by the time** 〜する時までに **for some time** しばらくの間 **for the first time** 初めて **have a hard time 〜ing** 〜するのに苦労する **have no time to do** 〜する時間がない

□ **tobacco** 名 たばこ

□ **toe** 名 足指, つま先

□ **tone** 名 音, 音色, 調子 動 調和する [させる]

□ **too** 熟 **too much** 過度に **too 〜 to** …・・・するには〜すぎる

□ **tool** 名 道具, 用具, 工具

□ **top** 名 ①頂上, 首位 ②こま 形 いちばん上の 動 ①頂上を覆う ②首位を占める ③(〜より) 優れる

□ **tore** 動 tear (裂く) の過去

□ **torn** 動 tear (裂く) の過去分詞

□ **total** 形 総計の, 全体の, 完全な 名 全体, 合計 動 合計する

□ **totally** 副 全体的に, すっかり

□ **touch** 動 ①触れる, さわる, 〜を触れさせる ②接触する ③感動させる 名 ①接触, 手ざわり ②手法

□ **translation** 名 翻訳, 言い換え, 解釈

□ **transportation** 名 交通 (機関), 輸送手段

□ **treasure** 名 財宝, 貴重品, 宝物 動 秘蔵する

□ **treat** 動 ①扱う ②治療する ③おごる 名 ①おごり, もてなし, ごちそう ②楽しみ

□ **trouble** 名 ①困難, 迷惑 ②心配, 苦労 ③もめごと 動 ①悩ます, 心配させる ②迷惑をかける

□ **true** 形 ①本当の, 本物の, 真の ②誠実な, 確かな 副 本当に, 心から

□ **truly** 副 ①全く, 本当に, 真に ②心から, 誠実に

□ **trunk** 名 ①幹, 胴 ②本体, 主要部分 ③トランク, 旅行かばん

□ **trust** 動 信用 [信頼] する, 委託する 名 信用, 信頼, 委託

□ **truth** 名 ①真理, 事実, 本当 ②誠実, 忠実さ **to tell the truth** 実は, 実を言えば

□ **tulip tree** ユリノキ《植物》

□ **turn** 熟 **as it turned out** 後でわかったことだが **in turn** 順番に, 立ち代わって **turn into** 〜に変わる **turn out** 〜と判明する, (結局〜に) なる **turn over** ひっくり返る [返す], (ページを) めくる, 思いめぐらす, 引き渡す **turn red** 赤くなる **turn to** 〜の方を向く, 〜に頼る, 〜に変わる **turn white** 青ざめる, 血の気が引く

□ **two-thirds** 名 3分の2

U

□ **unable** 形 《be – to 〜》〜することができない

□ **uncover** 動 ふたを取る, 覆いを取る

□ **understanding** 動 understand (理解する) の現在分詞 名 理解, 意見

142

WORD LIST

の一致, 了解 形 理解のある, 思いやりのある

□ **undertaker** 名 葬儀屋

□ **undertaking** 動 undertake (引き受ける)の現在分詞 名 (引き受けた)仕事, 事業

□ **underwent** 動 undergo (経験する)の過去

□ **unexpected** 形 思いがけない, 予期しない

□ **unexpectedly** 副 思いがけなく, 突然に

□ **unhappily** 副 不幸に, 運悪く, 不愉快そうに

□ **unknown** 形 知られていない, 不明の

□ **unlike** 形 似ていない, 違った **not unlike** ～とよく似ている 副 ～と違って

□ **unlucky** 形 ①不運な ②不吉な, 縁起の悪い

□ **unpleasant** 形 不愉快な, 気にさわる, いやな, 不快な

□ **unusual** 形 普通でない, 珍しい, 見[聞き]慣れない

□ **unwell** 形 気分が悪い

□ **up** 熟 **be made up of** ～で構成されている **come to pick up** ～を取りに来る **come up** 近づいてくる, 浮上する, 水面へ上ってくる **dig up** 掘り起こす, 掘り出す **get up** 起き上がる, 立ち上がる **give oneself up to** ～に身を委ねる **give up** あきらめる, やめる, 引き渡す **go up** ①～に上がる, 登る ②～に近づく, 出かける **go up to** ～まで行く, 近づく **look up** 見上げる, 調べる **make up** 作り出す, 考え出す, ～を構成[形成]する **make up one's mind** 決心する **pick up** 拾い上げる, 車で迎えに行く **push up** 押し上げる **stand up** 立ち上がる **up and down** 上がったり下がったり, 行ったり来たり, あちこちと **wake up** 起きる, 目を覚ます **walk up and down** 行ったり来たりする

□ **used** 動 ①use (使う)の過去, 過去分詞 ②《– to》よく～したものだ, 以前は～であった 形 ①慣れている, 《get [become]– to》～に慣れてくる ②使われた, 中古の

□ **usual** 形 通常の, いつもの, 平常の, 普通の **as usual** いつものように, 相変わらず **than usual** いつもより

V

□ **valley** 名 谷, 谷間

□ **valuable** 形 貴重な, 価値のある, 役に立つ

□ **value** 名 価値, 値打ち, 価格 動 評価する, 値をつける, 大切にする

□ **vegetation** 名 ①植物, 草木 ②植物の生長

□ **victory** 名 勝利, 優勝

□ **visible** 形 目に見える, 明らかな

□ **visitor** 名 訪問客

W

□ **wall** 名 ①壁, 塀 ②障壁 動 壁[塀]で囲む, ふさぐ

□ **walled** 形 壁のある, 城壁をめぐらした

□ **warm** 熟 **look like death warmed over** 死んだようにぐったりしている

□ **warmth** 名 暖かさ, 思いやり

□ **warn** 動 警告する, 用心させる

□ **waste** 動 浪費する, 消耗する 形 ①むだな, 余分な ②不毛の, 荒涼とした 名 ①浪費, 消耗 ②くず, 廃物 ③荒地

□ **watch over** 見守る, 見張る

□ **wave** 名 ①波 ②(手などを)振ること 動 ①揺れる, 揺らす, 波立つ ②(手などを振って)合図する

143

THE BEST SHORT STORIES OF EDGAR ALLAN POE

□ **way** 熟 all the way through 始めから終わりまで, 完全に by the way ところで, ついでに, 途中で give way to ～に変わる, 抑え切れずに～する have no way of doing ～するすべがない, ～しようがない in any way 決して, 多少なりとも in much the same way ほぼ同じように in no way 決して～でない in some way 何とかして, 何らかの方法で in this way このようにして lead the way 先に立って導く, 案内する, 率先する on one's way out 出ていくときに on the way home 帰宅途中に one's way through 押し分けて進む this way and that あちこちへ way out 出口, 逃げ道, 脱出方法, 解決法

□ **weakly** 形 病弱な, 弱々しい 副 弱々しく

□ **weakness** 名 ①弱さ, もろさ ②欠点, 弱点

□ **wealthy** 形 裕福な, 金持ちの

□ **wear** 動 ①着る, 着ている, 身につける ②疲れる, 消耗する, すり切れる wear on 経過する 名 ①着用 ②衣類

□ **weigh** 動 ①(重さを)はかる ②重さが～ある ③圧迫する, 重荷である weigh down (人)の気を重くさせる

□ **weight** 名 ①重さ, 重力, 体重 ②重荷, 負担 ③重大さ, 勢力 動 ①重みをつける ②重荷を負わせる

□ **well** 副 ①うまく, 上手に ②十分に, よく, かなり as well なお, その上, 同様に as well as ～と同様に be well -ed よく[十分に]～された may well ～するのももっともだ, 多分～だろう 間 へえ, まあ, ええと 形 健康な, 適当な, 申し分ない 名 井戸

□ **well-built** 形 しっかりした造りの

□ **what to make of** ～をどう判断するか

□ **whatsoever** 代 形 whatever (何であれ・いかなる～も)の強意

□ **whether** 接 ～かどうか, ～かまたは…, ～であろうとなかろうと

□ **while** 熟 for a while しばらくの間, 少しの間 once in a while たまに, 時々

□ **whip** 動 ①むちうつ ②急に動く[動かす] 名 むち

□ **whole** 形 全体の, すべての, 完全な, 満～, 丸～ 名 《the ‒》全体, 全部

□ **wide** 形 幅の広い, 広範囲の, 幅が～ある 副 広く, 大きく開いて

□ **widen** 動 広くなる[する], 大きく開く

□ **wild** 形 ①野生の ②荒涼として ③荒っぽい ④奇抜な

□ **wild-looking** 形 荒れた様子の

□ **will** 助 ～だろう, ～しよう, する(つもりだ) 名 決意, 意図

□ **William Bird** 名 ウィリアム・バード《人名》

□ **William Legrand** 名 ウィリアム・ルグラン《人名》

□ **willing** 形 ①喜んで～する, ～しても構わない, いとわない ②自分から進んで行う

□ **wine** 名 ワイン, ぶどう酒

□ **wing** 名 翼, 羽

□ **wise** 形 賢明な, 聡明な, 博学の

□ **wisely** 副 賢明に

□ **witch** 名 魔法使い, 魔女

□ **with** 前 ①《同伴・付随・所属》～と一緒に, ～を身につけて, ～とともに ②《様態》～(の状態)で, ～して ③《手段・道具》～で, ～を使って

□ **within** 前 ①～の中[内]に, ～の内部に ②～以内で, ～を越えないで 副 中[内]へ[に], 内部に 名 内部

□ **woke** 動 wake (目が覚める)の過去

□ **woken** 動 wake (目が覚める)の過去分詞

□ **wonder** 動 ①不思議に思う, (～に)驚く ②(～かしらと)思う 名 驚き(の念), 不思議なもの

□ **wooden** 形 木製の, 木でできた

144

WORD LIST

- [ ] **word** 名 ①語, 単語 ②ひと言 ③《one's ~》約束

- [ ] **wore** 動 wear（着ている）の過去

- [ ] **work** 動 ①働く, 勉強する, 取り組む ②機能［作用］する, うまくいく **work on** ～で働く, ～に取り組む 名 ①仕事, 勉強 ②職 ③作品 **fall to work** 仕事を始める

- [ ] **world** 名《the ~》世界, ～界

- [ ] **worn** 動 wear（着ている）の過去分詞 形 ①すり切れた, 使い古した ②やつれた, 疲れた **worn out** 疲れはてた

- [ ] **would** 助《will の過去》①～するだろう, ～するつもりだ ②《W- you ～?》～してくださいませんか ③～したものだ ④《否定文で》～しようとしなかった, どうしても～しなかった **would like to** ～したいと思う

- [ ] **wreckage** 名（難破船などの）残骸, がれき, 破片

- [ ] **wrong** 熟 **be wrong with**（～にとって）よくない, ～が故障している

Y

- [ ] **years** 熟 **for ～ years** ～年間, ～年にわたって

- [ ] **yet** 副 ①《否定文で》まだ～（ない［しない］） ②《疑問文で》もう ③《肯定文で》まだ, 今もなお 接《and yet とも》それにもかかわらず, しかし, けれども

145

English Conversational Ability Test
国際英語会話能力検定

● E-CATとは…

英語が話せるようになるための
テストです。インターネット
ベースで、30分であなたの発
話力をチェックします。

www.ecatexam.com

● iTEP®とは…

世界各国の企業、政府機関、アメリカの大学
300校以上が、英語能力判定テストとして採用。
オンラインによる90分のテストで文法、リー
ディング、リスニング、ライティング、スピー
キングの5技能をスコア化。iTEP®は、留学、就
職、海外赴任などに必要な、世界に通用する英
語力を総合的に評価する画期的なテストです。

www.itepexamjapan.com

ラダーシリーズ

The Best Short Stories of Edgar Allan Poe

エドガー・アラン・ポー名作選

2019年4月13日　第1刷発行
2022年7月4日　第2刷発行

原著者　エドガー・アラン・ポー

発行者　浦　　晋亮

発行所　**IBCパブリッシング株式会社**
〒162-0804　東京都新宿区中里町29番3号
菱秀神楽坂ビル
Tel. 03-3513-4511　Fax. 03-3513-4512
www.ibcpub.co.jp

© Michael Brase 2006, 2007
© IBC Publishing, Inc. 2019

印刷　株式会社シナノパブリッシングプレス
装丁　伊藤 理恵
カバーイラスト　Byam Shaw　本文イラスト　坂本ロクタク
組版データ　Berkeley Oldstyle Medium + Abadi MT Condensed Extra Regular

落丁本・乱丁本は、小社宛にお送りください。送料小社負担にてお取り替えいたし
ます。本書の無断複写(コピー)は著作権法上での例外を除き禁じられています。

Printed in Japan
ISBN978-4-7946-0576-4